Haley, Alex

The Autobiography of Malcolm X

DEMCO

IN SYSTEM

Bloom's
GUIDES

Alex Haley's
The Autobiography of Malcolm X

The Adventures of Huckleberry Finn
All the Pretty Horses
Animal Farm
The Autobiography of Malcolm X
The Awakening
Beloved
Beowulf
Brave New World
The Canterbury Tales
The Catcher in the Rye
The Chosen
The Crucible
Cry, the Beloved Country
Death of a Salesman
Fahrenheit 451
Frankenstein
The Glass Menagerie
The Grapes of Wrath
Great Expectations
The Great Gatsby
Hamlet
The Handmaid's Tale
The House on Mango Street
I Know Why the Caged Bird Sings
The Iliad
Invisible Man
Jane Eyre

Lord of the Flies
Macbeth
Maggie: A Girl of the Streets
The Member of the Wedding
The Metamorphosis
Native Son
1984
The Odyssey
Oedipus Rex
Of Mice and Men
One Hundred Years of Solitude
Pride and Prejudice
Ragtime
The Red Badge of Courage
Romeo and Juliet
The Scarlet Letter
A Separate Peace
Slaughterhouse-Five
Snow Falling on Cedars
The Stranger
A Streetcar Named Desire
The Sun Also Rises
A Tale of Two Cities
The Things They Carried
To Kill a Mockingbird
Uncle Tom's Cabin
The Waste Land
Wuthering Heights

Bloom's
GUIDES

Alex Haley's
The Autobiography of Malcolm X

Edited & with an Introduction
by Harold Bloom

BLOOM'S
LITERARY CRITICISM
An imprint of Infobase Publishing

Bloom's Guides: The Autobiography of Malcolm X

Copyright © 2008 by Infobase Publishing

Introduction © 2008 by Harold Bloom

Bloom's Literary Criticism
An imprint of Infobase Publishing
132 West 31st Street
New York, NY 10001

Library of Congress Cataloging-in-Publication Data
Bloom, Harold.
  Alex Haley's The autobiography of Malcolm X / Harold Bloom.
    p. cm. — (Bloom's guides)
  Includes bibliographical references and index.
  ISBN 978-0-7910-9832-5 (hardcover)
  1. X, Malcolm, 1925–1965. Autobiography of Malcolm X.
  2. African American Muslims—Biography. 3. Haley, Alex. I. Title.
  II. Title: Autobiography of Malcolm X. III. Series.

  BP223.Z8B56 2008
  320.54'6092—dc22
  [B]

                                           2007051313

Contributing Editor: Amy Sickels
Cover design by Takeshi Takahashi
Printed in the United States of America
Bang EJB 10 9 8 7 6 5 4 3 2 1
This book is printed on acid-free paper.

Contents

Introduction

HAROLD BLOOM

Even as I write these brief remarks about this still vital document, the United States may be setting forth finally to mend the abyss that Malcolm X proudly represented. Barack Obama has just won the Iowa primary, and I desperately hope for his nomination and election. A nation and a world in need of healing could not do better than Obama. Our presidency is imperial, as George W. Bush demonstrates daily, and to place such power in Obama would guarantee a benign reign ahead of us.

Malcolm X, in the perspective of the twenty-first century, is a crucial figure in American cultural history. The Nation of Islam is now mostly within the safe confines of Orthodox Sunni Islam, which recognizes no distinctions between blacks and whites. Had Malcolm X not been murdered, we do not know where he would have turned his spiritual and political energies. It is very dubious that he would have converted to Sunni Islam, but nothing about this remarkable man was predictable.

There are no literary standards that would be relevant to *The Autobiography of Malcolm X*, but Haley was bearing witness and was not guided by aesthetic motivations. Richard Wright's *Black Boy* seems to me a work of considerable aesthetic merit, superior to the novelist's *Native Son*. But Malcolm X was something different, a man working out his own mission in the conviction that it might help save his people. His fierce individualism is in an American tradition that goes back to John Brown, who rightly believed that only violence could end American slavery. It is a long road from the martyrdoms of John Brown and Malcolm X to the advent of Barack Obama, and Haley's document is an important tracing of part of that road.

Biographical Sketch

Malcolm X was born Malcolm Little on May 19, 1925, in Omaha, Nebraska, to Earl and Louise Little. He was his father's seventh child and his mother's fourth (Earl had three children from a previous marriage). His father was a Baptist minister who advocated the philosophy of Marcus Garvey, a Black Nationalist who urged African Americans to return to Africa. Threatened by white supremacists, the Little family moved several times and settled in Lansing, Michigan. In 1931 Malcolm's father was viciously beaten by a white mob and run over by a trolley train. His killers were never brought to justice. Malcolm's mother struggled to raise the children on her own, but she suffered a nervous breakdown and was institutionalized. The children were split up among various families and orphanages.

Malcolm attended a predominately white school in Lansing and excelled—he was a smart, popular student. However, when he told a teacher that he wanted to be a lawyer, he was advised that, because of his race, this was not a realistic goal. Malcolm grew disillusioned with the white-dominated environment. He dropped out of school and moved to Boston, living with his half-sister Ella. Malcolm became seduced by the city's nightlife and began drinking, gambling, and dabbling in drugs.

In late 1941 Malcolm moved to Harlem, in New York City, joining the underworld of drug dealing, gambling, prostitution, and armed robbery. He was arrested for and convicted of burglary in 1946. While in prison, Malcolm's siblings introduced him to the Nation of Islam, a Black Muslim religious sect that preached black separatism and resistance to white oppression.

Malcolm embraced the religion. He stopped using drugs, prayed, studied, read voraciously, and entered into debates spawned by his new ideology. When he was released from prison in 1952, he became a devoted follower of Elijah Muhammad, the leader of the Nation of Islam. Malcolm accepted the basic argument that evil was an inherent characteristic of the "white man's Christian world" and believed that, through Islam, African Americans would be able to achieve economic, political, and social success.

Malcolm adopted the surname X and quickly became one of Elijah's most persuasive and vocal ministers. He established several mosques in different cities and actively sought publicity to promote the teachings of the Nation. In 1958 he married Betty (Sanders) X; they would have six daughters.

Malcolm delivered spellbinding speeches on the street corners of Harlem and other urban centers, and the Nation of Islam's membership increased by the thousands. Malcolm's provocative debates on panels and his lectures to predominantly white college audiences helped to build his reputation as the most controversial figure of the civil rights movement. He became known throughout the United States as a fiery advocate for black unity and militancy. He distanced himself from other civil rights leaders, such as Martin Luther King, Jr., who advocated peaceful forms of resistance. Malcolm X urged African Americans to use "any means necessary" to combat racism. Malcolm's fame eventually eclipsed that of his mentor, Elijah Muhammad.

In 1962 Alex Haley reported on Malcolm and the Nation and then approached Malcolm to write his autobiography. For two years, he interviewed Malcolm. Then in 1963 Malcolm X was devastated to learn that Elijah Muhammad, his spiritual leader, had committed adultery, breaking the rules of his faith. Shortly after, Malcolm X made a controversial comment following the assassination of President Kennedy, and Elijah Muhammad "silenced" him for ninety days. Hearing rumors that someone in the Nation had ordered his death, in March 1964 Malcolm X terminated his relationship with the Nation of Islam and founded the Muslim Mosque, Inc.

That same year, Malcolm went on a life-changing pilgrimage to Islam's holy city, Mecca, where he encountered what he believed was "true" Islam embraced the tenets of the religion's Sunni branch. With this transformation, he adopted the name El-Hajj Malik El Shabazz. He returned to the United States with changed views—that not all whites were evil, and that people of African descent around the world should unite. By then an international figure, he created the secular group the Organization of Afro-American Unity to promote black unity. His increased popularity and political activity also earned him many enemies. He was under surveillance by the local and federal authorities, while the relations between Malcolm and the Nation of Islam grew more volatile. On February 14, 1965, his home was firebombed, the family luckily escaping without injury.

A week later, on February 21, at a speaking engagement at Manhattan's Audubon Ballroom, three gunmen, allegedly Black Muslims, rushed Malcolm onstage and killed him. He was thirty-nine years old. More than twenty thousand mourners viewed his body, and fifteen hundred people attended the funeral in Harlem. At the time of his murder, Malcolm's views were undergoing a great change. Now he is remembered as one of the most well-known black leaders, recalled for his fights for civil rights, and often cited as the spiritual father of the Black Power movement in the late 1960s. The legacy of Malcolm X continues to permeate society—he is the subject of numerous books, documentaries, academic studies, and a notable feature film, Spike Lee's *Malcolm X* (1992), which starred Denzel Washington in the title role.

The Story Behind the Story

The Autobiography of Malcolm X was published in 1965 to much popular and critical acclaim. More than thirty years later, in 1999, *Time* magazine selected *The Autobiography* as one of the top ten nonfiction works of the twentieth century, placing it with classics such as *The Diary of Anne Frank.*

The book was written by Alex Haley (who would later write the best-selling *Roots*), based on a series of long interviews conducted with his subject between 1964 and 1965. Haley first became aware of the Nation of Islam in 1959, after the airing of a television segment "The Hate That Hate Produced." He spent time in Harlem collecting material, and after publishing a few articles on the Black Muslims and Malcolm X, in 1963 a publisher asked him to write a book about Malcolm's life. When Haley approached Malcolm with the idea, Malcolm gave him a startled look: "It was one of the few times I have ever seen him uncertain." After Malcolm received permission from Elijah Muhammad, he and Haley began the process— two- and three-hour sessions in which Malcolm would visit Haley's studio in Greenwich Village. Haley admitted, "We got off to a very poor start." Malcolm was critical of Haley's middle-class status, as well as his Christian beliefs and twenty years of service in the U.S. military. Haley wondered if he should give up, as he had nothing in his notebook except for "Black Muslim philosophy, praise of Mr. Muhammad, and the evils of the 'the white devil.'" But one night, while Malcolm was proselytizing, Haley interrupted, "I wonder if you'd tell me something about your mother?" Posing the question proved to be the turning point in their collaboration. Haley began to build a foundation for the book, as he learned about Malcolm's childhood.

During the years that Haley interviewed Malcolm, the civil rights movement was gaining power and momentum, and the atmosphere in America was turbulent and volatile. Through peaceful means, civil rights leader Martin Luther King, Jr., the Freedom Riders, and thousands of people across the country were fighting to put an end to the legalized racism that infused American life, especially in the South. Malcolm X also spent much of his life fighting for equal rights for African Americans, but he distanced himself from the mainstream civil rights leaders. Malcolm believed in separatism and militancy and disdained nonviolent philosophies. During this period, he gained national and international prominence and also became known as the most controversial man in America, seen by many as "the only Negro in America who could either start a race riot—or stop one."

When Malcolm agreed to write the book with Haley, he expected to use it as a means to publicize the teachings of Elijah Muhammad and the Nation of Islam. He originally dedicated the book to Elijah and demanded that the profits be turned over to the Nation. However, in 1964, Malcolm split with the Nation, amid growing tensions and the revelation of Elijah Muhammad's marital infidelity.

When Malcolm made his momentous pilgrimage to Mecca, he experienced a profound spiritual upheaval and returned to America with a radically different perspective, including a new belief that whites were not inherently evil. Understanding that the book, like life, was a work in progress, Malcolm appropriately asked Haley, "How is it possible to write one's autobiography in a world so fast-changing as this?" By the end of his life, Malcolm was focused on securing human rights for African Americans by developing unity among oppressed peoples around the world. Malcolm predicted he would not live to see the book published. He died on February 21, 1965, and the book was published later that year.

Because of the unusual double authorship, critics have addressed concerns of authenticity. Though Haley was one of the most famous African American authors of the twentieth century, his work has been questioned for its scholarly integrity, with critics charging that *Roots* was poorly researched. A majority of critics, however, have viewed Haley's role in the autobiography as vital, deeming it a book of distinction. Forty years later, Malcolm's words still resonate. By the late 1990s, nearly three million copies of the work had been sold worldwide.

Forty years after his death, Malcolm X continues to be a source of controversy and inspiration. Many regard him as the force behind the Black Power movement in the late 1960s, and by the late 1980s, Malcolm X began to emerge as a cultural icon. This popularity has continued to swell, with many prominent hip-hop artists drawing on his words and image in their works. In 1992 director Spike Lee adapted the *Autobiography* for his film *Malcolm X*, renewing interest in the title subject around the world. Most black historians rank Malcolm X among the most influential personalities in African American history, a powerful group that includes Frederick Douglass, Booker T. Washington, W.E.B. Du Bois, Marcus Garvey, and Martin Luther King, Jr.

The Autobiography of Malcolm X, still relevant today, is an important book that documents the African American struggle for equality and justice and tells the story of a remarkable man who evolved from anger and ignorance to spiritual, political, and intellectual enlightenment.

List of Characters

Malcolm X is the narrator and subject of the autobiography. Born Malcolm Little, he grows up in a large family that is split up after his father's death and mother's breakdown. After a crime-tinged life in Boston and Harlem, he is sentenced to prison for armed robbery. There he embraces the Muslim faith and adopts X as his surname. Charismatic, intelligent, and fiery, Malcolm is devoted to the Nation of Islam and becomes the group's best-known and most persuasive speaker. After Nation leader Elijah Muhammad betrays his Muslim ideals, however, Malcolm X breaks with the Nation and makes a pilgrimage to Mecca, where he undergoes a profound transformation. He begins to advocate pan-Africanism, his political views evolving and becoming more inclusive as he fights for human rights and justice for African Americans.

Alex Haley, the author, spent two years interviewing Malcolm. He includes an epilogue to the book, in which he further develops Malcolm's character and addresses the period leading up to Malcolm's death and its aftermath. It is the only time in the book that he shares his particular viewpoint.

Elijah Muhammad is the spiritual leader of the Nation of Islam. A father figure who takes Malcolm under his wing, Elijah Muhammad teaches Malcolm the Nation's theology and history. He appoints Malcolm as his spokesman but then tries to rein him in after Malcolm's influence grows. Malcolm is devastated to learn that Elijah has committed adultery and had children out of wedlock, violating the tenets of his faith. Elijah tries to silence Malcolm and allegedly orders other Muslims to kill Malcolm.

Sister Betty is Malcolm's wife, a supportive, devoted, and patient mother of six. One of the few women Malcolm has ever trusted, she witnesses his assassination.

Ella Little is Malcolm's half-sister on his father's side. She is a strong, assertive woman, a symbol of black pride. She constantly supports Malcolm, arranging for him to live with her in Boston and later financing his pilgrimage to Mecca.

Shorty, an aspiring musician, is Malcolm's best friend in Boston. He gives Malcolm his first "conk" or hair straightening, gets him a job as a shoeshine boy, and teaches him the ways of the neighborhood. Later, he and Malcolm commit robberies and are sentenced to prison.

Earl Little is Malcolm's father. He is a Baptist minister and an advocate of Marcus Garvey's "Back to Africa" philosophy. An outspoken, imposing authority figure and a target of white racist groups for his activism, he is savagely beaten and killed in 1931.

Louise Little is Malcolm's mother, an educated woman. She is a West Indian woman who is often mistaken as white. She loses jobs when her employers discover that she is black. After the death of her husband, she struggles to support her eight children. Welfare agents separate her from her children, and she enters a mental hospital, where she remains for almost twenty-six years.

Sophia is Malcolm's white girlfriend, who he meets at a dance in Boston. For Malcolm, she is initially a status symbol. Later, she comes to represent the tempting allure of the white woman that can lead to a black man's downfall, and his evolving perceptions of their relationship fuel his argument against interracial marriage.

Laura is a quiet, intelligent, middle-class black woman from Roxbury Hill. She talks with Malcolm at the soda shop, and although they start a tentative relationship and go to dances at Roseland, Malcolm leaves her for Sophia. Later, Laura becomes a drug addict and prostitute, a turn of events for which Malcolm blames himself.

Sammy the Pimp is Malcolm's closest friend in Harlem. He is a pimp and drug dealer. Malcolm and Sammy work together, hustling and committing robberies.

West Indian Archie is an older Harlem hustler who runs a gambling ring. He and Malcolm violently split over a misunderstanding. Archie's sharp memory and math skills exemplify the way potential is wasted in those barred from opportunity or the chance to develop strengths and talents.

Bimbi is a prison inmate who is well read and speaks to the prisoners and the guards about a range of subjects. He encourages Malcolm to read and to enroll in the prison correspondence courses.

Cassius Clay (Muhammad Ali) was a friend of Malcolm's before his split with Elijah. The world heavyweight boxing champion converted to Islam and was loved by Muslims around the world. He gives Malcolm a place to stay during the first days of Malcolm's split from the Nation of Islam.

Reginald Little is one of Malcolm's younger brothers. While Malcolm is in prison, Reginald urges him to convert to Islam. When Reginald is suspended from the Nation for "improper relations" with a secretary, Malcolm struggles with this decision but finally supports Elijah Muhammad instead of his brother. After the Muslims expel Reginald, he experiences a mental breakdown.

Wilfred Little is Malcolm's oldest brother and one of the people who urges him to convert. Wilfred remains a minister for the Nation of Islam even after Malcolm has broken with the organization.

Summary and Analysis

1

The Autobiography of Malcolm X is the result of the collaboration between political activist Malcolm X and the writer Alex Haley (author of the best-selling *Roots*). Over two years and many interviews, Malcolm X told his story to Haley, who shaped the material into a book. Haley writes in the first-person point of view, giving readers the impression that Malcolm is speaking directly to them. While this unusual authorship has provoked questions about accuracy and authenticity, most critics agree the final result is a rich, complex, personal narrative that could not have been possible without such a collaboration.

Haley vividly portrays Malcolm X's momentous journey, the spiritual and political transformations that lead to a profound awakening. The autobiography follows a series of significant changes in Malcolm's life, each one marked by his assuming a different name. The first phase concerns Malcolm's childhood and adolescence, when he is known as Malcolm Little, member of a strict Baptist family. The first major change occurs in Chapter 3, when he leaves Michigan for Boston, where he takes on the persona Homeboy, and for the first time in his life, lives in a large African American neighborhood. Chapters 5 through 10 document his "downfall" in Harlem, where he is known as Detroit Red. In Chapter 10, in prison, he is called Satan, symbolizing his anger and antireligious attitude. Then Malcolm is introduced to the teachings of the Nation of Islam, and in Chapter 11 "Saved," he experiences a major religious and intellectual transformation. After he converts to the Nation of Islam, he replaces his surname with X. Chapters 10 through 15 document his life as a minister for the Nation of Islam.

The autobiography follows the traditional structure of a conversion narrative; Malcolm falls as low as he can go, then is "saved." According to critic Paul Eakin,

> If we consider Malcolm X's account of his life up to the time of his break with Elijah Muhammad . . . what we have

in fact is a story that falls rather neatly into two sections roughly equal in length, devoted respectively to his former life as a sinner (Chapters 3–9) and to his present life as one of Elijah Muhammad's ministers (Chapters 10–15). (p. 154).

Yet as Eakin argues, the narrative then takes the traditional conversion narrative one step further. After Malcolm leaves the Nation of Islam, he goes on a pilgrimage to Mecca, where he embraces "true Islam" and changes his name to El-Hajj Malik El-Shabazz as a way to mark this radical transformation. In Chapters 18 and 19, he tries to rise above his old image as the controversial minister of the Nation of Islam, as he evolves into a more open-minded revolutionary; however, before this transformation can be completed, he is tragically murdered. Haley includes an epilogue, completing the chronology of Malcolm's life and providing information about his death and its aftermath.

Each transformation reveals another aspect of Malcolm's character. Sometimes the changes contrast one another, but as critic Bashir El-Beshti points out, "Malcolm might seem like a different man in each of his incarnations, but his essence—of fluidity, of emergence, of growth—always remains intact" (p. 363). Despite the many stages of his life, the narrative voice also remains consistent. It is a detached, even-toned, and authorial voice that is still laced with anger and is often moralizing. For example, he provides political commentary about something he experienced earlier in his life, such as the conk: "Malcolm, the authorial voice, the mature, integrated human being, frequently interrupts the story being told to direct our attention to one didactic point or another" (El-Beshti, p. 359). At the same time, Malcolm shows an ability to laugh at himself, as with the outlandish zoot suit. Despite his self-awareness and the lectures to his audience, usually what Malcolm condemns later in life does not detract from the vivid descriptions offered of his rise and transformation, including his portrayal of lindy-hopping and of hustling. As critic David Demarest, Jr. points out, "Malcolm relives it all in retrospect, not for a moment falling into the moralizer's trap of turning what he condemns into clay pigeons" (p. 183). The result is that the early scenes in Boston and Harlem jump to life, and many critics consider them the most vivid in the book.

The *Autobiography* documents the history of race relations in America, with a focus on religion and politics. Malcolm offers his lifestory "as a parable," suggests El-Beshti: "It is important for Malcolm, however, to stress that he is not unique; he is a black man who shares his experience with other black men" (p. 362). And yet, more than a record of the times, the book provides psychological insight into a fascinating figure. "Malcolm comes through as a man who was above all bent on discovering and expanding himself to his fullest limits," attests Demarest (p. 187). The reader is occasionally offered a glimpse of the vulnerability that lies behind Malcolm's fiery rhetoric and confidence. He is a complex character—fearless and dogmatic, yet willing to change.

2

The first two chapters chronicle Malcolm's upbringing, how the early uncertainties and chaos will lead him on a lifelong quest for order and wholeness. The book begins in violence: While Malcolm's mother is pregnant with him, "a party of hooded Ku Klux Klan riders galloped up to our home in Omaha, Nebraska, one night" looking for his father. His father's separatist views provoke white hostility wherever the family goes. Thus, by beginning with this scene, Malcolm shows how early experiences shape his understanding of racism in the United States. He establishes the violence of racism and his formation of his views on "the good Christian white people" who run them out of town.

Malcolm describes his family in Chapter 1, "Nightmare." Malcolm's father, Earl Little, is a tall imposing man from Georgia. He is a Baptist preacher and an organizer for Marcus Garvey's Universal Negro Improvement Association (U.N.I.A.). Marcus Garvey was a proponent of the "back to Africa" movement, and Earl Little spreads his philosophy "that freedom, independence and self-respect could never be achieved by the Negro in America, and that therefore the

Negro should leave America to the white man and return to his African land of origin." Later, under the guidance of Elijah Muhammad, Malcolm will adopt beliefs similar to his father's. Malcolm stresses his father's political views more so than he does his father's Christian faith, in order to draw a connection between these early influences and his own political vision.

Malcolm is born May 19, 1925, in Omaha, Nebraska. He is the fourth child of his father and mother (his father also has three children from a previous marriage); following his birth, his mother will have four more children. As the lightest-skinned child in the family, Malcolm is the only one who escapes his father's beatings. Malcolm relates this personal experience to portray how deeply racism runs in America—that even a black man, an advocate of African American pride, favors light skin. Malcolm's mother, Louise Little, however, is harder on Malcolm than the other children for the same reason—his light skin. His mother, born in Grenada (the British West Indies), is able to be perceived by many as white. Malcolm looks like her, but she "favored the [children] that were darker," which he believes is because his skin reminds her of her white father: "I learned to hate every drop of that white rapist's blood that is in me."

Soon after his birth, the family moves briefly to Milwaukee, Wisconsin, to escape threats of white violence, then on to Lansing, Michigan, where his father encounters trouble with a white supremacist group called the Black Legion, a "local hate society." One night in 1929, "the nightmare night," the mob sets the Littles' house on fire. The family must move two miles out of town, to a place where Malcolm "really begin[s] to remember things—this home where I started to grow up."

When Malcolm is six years old, his father is killed, most likely by members of the Black Legion. Malcolm claims that after beating him savagely, the murderers laid his body over the streetcar tracks, where it was then crushed. Despite the incriminating details of his death, an insurance company rules it suicide and refuses to pay off the policy. As the country plunges into the Great Depression, Louise must raise eight children on her own, without any financial support. Passing as white, she takes on work as a housekeeper, but once her employers discover that she is black, she is fired. Malcolm observes how his mother's light skin provides her with opportunities but that she is also a victim of a racist society, her duel heritage making her an outsider to both cultures.

Unable to make ends meet, the family has no choice but to go on welfare, which proves to be a devastating experience. His mother, under great stress, is harassed by the white welfare workers, though she tries to stand up for herself: "What I later learned was that my mother was making a desperate effort to preserve her pride—and ours. Pride was just about all we had to preserve." By 1934, when Malcolm is nine years old, the family is destitute. Sometimes they have nothing to eat but boiled dandelion greens.

His mother joins the Seventh-day Adventists, "the friendliest white people I had ever seen." When Louise refuses to feed her family pork, following the Seventh-day Adventists' doctrine, the social workers call her crazy. Malcolm recalls, "We children watched our anchor giving way. It was something terrible that you couldn't get your hands on, yet you couldn't get away from. It was a sensing that something bad was going to happen."

Harassed by the social workers and overwhelmed by the burden of trying to take care of eight children under such dire circumstances, Louise suffers a nervous breakdown and is committed to a state mental institution, where she remains for twenty-five years. For Malcolm, the role the state agency plays in breaking up his family becomes symbolic of how deeply racism is ingrained in society and its institutions: "I truly believe that if ever a state social agency destroyed a family, it destroyed ours. We wanted and tried to stay together. Our home didn't have to be destroyed."

These early chapters set the stage for the political and religious beliefs that Malcolm will later embrace. As a child, Malcolm sees that his father is killed for promoting a strong, independent black community, while his mother is driven crazy by a white agency that does not trust her to take care of her own children. Malcolm's world spirals into chaos at a young age; he has lost both his mother and father and is separated from his siblings.

At thirteen years old, in Chapter 2, "Mascot," Malcolm finds temporary order when he is sent to live with a white foster family in Lansing. He recalls the Swerlins as "good people." Except for the church dinners with the Seventh-day Adventists, this is first time that Malcolm has dined with white people. The Swerlins "liked my attitude, and it was out of their liking for me that I soon became accepted by them—as a mascot, I know now." The Swerlins and their friends would talk freely about "niggers," using hurtful language, "as though I wasn't there." The racist language is such a part of the culture that the Swerlins never think twice about it: "What I am trying to say is that it just never dawned upon them that I could understand, that I wasn't a pet, but a human being."

Malcolm attends the nearly all-white Mason Junior High School, an experience that resembles living with the Swerlins. The teachers and kids are friendly to him, and he is well liked, but only within the structures of a racist system. For example, when he plays basketball, the opponents' fans call him racist names, yet this type of language is so embedded in the social fabric that "It didn't bother my teammates or my coach at all, and to tell the truth, it bothered me only vaguely." And though he attends the school dances, he does not dance with the white girls: "Even at our school, I could sense it almost as a physical barrier, that despite all the beaming and smiling, the mascot wasn't supposed to dance with any of the white girls." The other boys often encourage him to approach the girls, but Malcolm understands it is an illusion. Though Malcolm is aware that "race-mixing went on in Lansing," it occurs secretively and only in certain parts of town.

Malcolm never feels threatened by the white students: "I was in fact extremely popular—I suppose partly because I was kind of a novelty. I was in demand. I had top priority." In seventh grade, Malcolm is elected class president: "I was unique in my class, like a pink poodle. And I was proud; I'm not going to say I wasn't." The choice of the image, "pink poodle," captures Malcolm's feeling that a black student making achievements in a white school is perceived as odd yet harmless. As a "pink poodle," Malcolm is a tame, obedient creature who poses no real threat; neither his friends, teachers, nor foster parents see him as a complex person with real goals. The color pink also symbolizes Malcolm's feelings of emasculation—his belief that white society strips black men of their manhood and autonomy.

When Malcolm's half-sister Ella visits from Boston, she leaves a strong impression on him, as she was "the first really proud black woman I had ever seen in my life." When Ella suggests that Malcolm spend his summer in Boston, "I jumped at that chance." In the summer of 1940, Malcolm boards the Greyhound bus with "my cardboard suitcase, and wearing my green suit. If someone had hung a sign, "HICK," around my neck, I couldn't have looked much more obvious." From "the back of the bus, I gawked out of the window at white man's America rolling past."

He discovers that Ella is active in clubs and "black society," living in the Sugar Hill section of Roxbury, "the Harlem of Boston." Malcolm is immediately drawn to the largely black population and the urban setting: "Neon lights, nightclubs, pool halls, bars, the cars they drove! Restaurants made the streets smell—rich, greasy, down-home black cooking!"

When he returns to Lansing, he misses Boston, where for the first time he experienced "the sense of being a real part of a mass of my own kind." Now, back to being a minority, a "pink poodle," he feels restless and out of place. These feelings deepen after a meeting with his English teacher, Mr. Ostrowski, an encounter that would "become the first major turning point of my life." His teacher asks Malcolm if he has been thinking about a career, and Malcolm replies that he is considering becoming a lawyer. Mr. Ostrowski is surprised. Though Malcolm is one of his "top students," he tells him, "you've got to be realistic about being a nigger," and he suggests that he become a carpenter.

The scene symbolizes the end of Malcolm's boyhood, shattering his belief that he will have the same opportunities as his white classmates: "It was then that I began to change—inside." The Swerlins sense that something is wrong, but

Malcolm does not know how to explain his new feelings. Instead he writes to Ella every day, and she arranges for custody of him. Malcolm explains, "I've thought about that time a lot since then. No physical move in my life has been more pivotal or profound in its repercussions."

3

Chapters 3 and 4 vividly portray Malcolm's transformation from a quiet, midwestern boy to a street-smart urban dweller. No longer the boy Malcolm Little, he quickly transforms into "Homeboy." When he first arrives in Boston in Chapter 3, he looks out of place: "Mason, Michigan was written all over me. My kinky, reddish hair was cut hick style, and I didn't even use grease in it. My green suit's coat sleeves stopped above my wrists, the pants leg showed three inches of socks." In addition to his many names, Malcolm uses clothes and physical appearance as symbols of his various transformations.

When Ella encourages him to go exploring before tying himself down to a job, Malcolm happily wanders all over Boston, to white downtown, the piers, and the black neighborhoods. Throughout the book, Malcolm criticizes the black middle class, a view that begins to develop when he is in Boston, as he observes the differences in Roxbury and the ghetto neighborhood. He feels irritated by African Americans in Roxbury Hill, inflating their status as security guards, janitors, and servants, and looking down on the poor. Malcolm claims that he feels more comfortable with the African Americans who live down the hill: "That world of grocery stores, walk-up flats, cheap restaurants, poolrooms, bars, storefront churches, and pawnshops seemed to hold a natural lure for me." Until prison, Malcolm does not form any kind of political ideology, but his early experiences are crucial in shaping it, as he observes the varied structures of oppression and levels of economic injustice.

Malcolm feels drawn to the "sharp-dressed cats" who wear their hair "straight and shiny like white men's hair." At a poolroom, he meets Shorty, an aspiring saxophonist. When the two start talking, they discover they are both from Lansing.

Shorty takes Malcolm under his wing and helps him get a job as a shoeshine boy at the Roseland State Ballroom. Malcolm soon realizes the job is more about hustling than shining shoes; his duties include putting white "johns" in touch with black prostitutes and selling liquor and "reefers." Malcolm likes being a part of the scene, where bandleaders such as Duke Ellington, Lionel Hampton, and Cootie Williams perform. He quickly embraces this new lifestyle—he shoots craps, plays cards, gambles, drinks, smokes, and uses drugs. He buys his first zoot suit, an outlandish and fashionable suit, and gets his first "conk," a style in which the hair is straightened. The ingredients for a conk include "Red Devil lye, two eggs, and two medium-sized white potatoes." When Shorty combs the toxic mixture into Malcolm's hair, it feels like "my head caught fire." Though the burning is nearly unbearable, afterward Malcolm stares in the mirror, staggered by the transformation: "The mirror reflected Shorty behind me. We both were grinning and sweating. And on top of my head was this thick, smooth sheen of shining red hair—real red—as straight as any white man's."

The conk symbolizes the pressure in American society for African Americans to emulate and imitate whites. Malcolm vividly describes the conk, capturing the humor of the moment, but also provides a sharp analysis:

> This was my first really big step toward self-degradation: when I endured all of that pain, literally burning my flesh to have it look like a white man's hair. I had joined that multitude of Negro men and women in America who are brainwashed into believing that the black people are 'inferior'—and white people 'superior'—that they will even violate and mutilate their God-created bodies to try to look 'pretty' by white standards.

Though Malcolm is critical of the middle-class blacks for imitating whites, he later realizes his conk is a symptom of the same kind of self-defacement. The conk represents a loss of black identity and serves as a distraction from the real problems of exploitation and oppression. He attests, "I admire any Negro man who has never had himself conked, or who has had the sense to get rid of it—as I finally did."

In Chapter 4 "Laura," Malcolm completes the transformation from the naïve boy in Lansing, Michigan, to "talking the slang like a lifelong hipster." At first, Malcolm is shy about dancing, but one night at a party, it "was as though somebody had clicked on a light." He buys a second zoot suit, "sharkskin gray, with a big, long coat, and pants ballooning out at the knees and then tapering down to cuffs so narrow that I had to take off my shoes to get them on and off," and he quits his shoeshining job. Now he only goes to the Roseland as a paying customer and never misses a dance, becoming one of the neighborhood's best lindy-hop dancers.

Ella, who does not approve of Malcolm's habits, gets him a job working as a soda fountain clerk in Roxbury. Malcolm feels uncomfortable and resentful of the middle-class black customers. But then he meets Laura, studious, quiet, and usually reading a book: "Watching her made me reflect that I hadn't even read a newspaper since leaving Mason." The two begin talking regularly: "She was certainly the only Hill girl that came in there and acted in any way friendly and natural." Malcolm tells her that he used to want to be a lawyer, and she does not laugh but encourages him to go after his dream.

When Malcolm asks Laura to a dance at the Roseland, he wears his most "conservative" suit and notices how Ella approves of his date. He is surprised that Laura is such a good dancer. When they go on a second date, they emerge as the stars of the dance floor: "Partly it was my reputation, and partly Laura's ballet style of dancing that helped to turn the spotlight—and the crowd's attention—to us." After the dance, they are swarmed by an admiring crowd. But then a white woman approaches Malcolm: "It's shameful to admit, but I had just about forgotten Laura."

Malcolm proceeds to dump Laura for Sophia, the white woman. He does not love Sophia but uses her as a way to improve his social standing in the eyes of his friends: "it was when I began to be seen around town with Sophia that I really began to mature into some real status in black downtown Roxbury."

Laura never comes back to the soda shop, and soon after, Malcolm quits. Years later, he discovers that Laura has "fallen" from her innocence: "[S]he was a wreck of a woman, notorious around black Roxbury, in and out of jail." Malcolm feels guilty and blames himself for exposing her to the underworld: "To have treated her as I did for a white woman made the blow doubly heavy." Laura becomes symbolic of the way an exploitive environment can gravely harm a respectable person, and he views her as one of the many victims of a racist society.

4

In Chapter 5, "Harlemite," Malcolm gets a job on the railroad, first as a dishwasher, then as a porter. Much to Ella's disappointment, he also continues to see Sophia. His first train trip is to Washington, D.C., which leaves a strong impression on him, though at the time he is unable to articulate his feelings:

> I was astounded to find in the nation's capital, just a few blocks from Capitol Hill, thousands of Negroes living worse than any I'd ever seen in the poorest sections of Roxbury; in dirt-floor shacks along unspeakably filthy lanes with names like Pig Alley and Goat Alley.... [s]tumblebums, pushers, hookers, public crap-shooters, even little kids running around at midnight begging for pennies, half-naked and barefooted . . . just a few blocks from the White House.

This is one of many observations that will later contribute to shaping his ideology.

After a few runs to Washington, D.C., he works on the "Yankee Clipper" and makes his first trip to New York: "I was into my zoot suit before the first passenger got off." In Harlem, his first stop is Small's Paradise, a well-known nightclub. He notices the men gathered around the circular bar are conservatively dressed, quiet, well mannered, and evoke a sense of power: "No Negro place of business had ever impressed me so much." He learns later that the men in Smalls are in the "numbers" business, representing "the cream of the older, more mature operators in Harlem."

Malcolm is dazzled by New York: "Within the first five minutes in Small's, I had left Boston and Roxbury forever." He visits the Savoy Ballroom, the Apollo Theater, and the Braddock Hotel, all Harlem hangouts that attracted well-known musicians such as Dizzy Gillespie, Billie Holiday, Ella Fitzgerald, and Dinah Washington. He feels like he has found his place: "But that night I was mesmerized. This world was where I belonged. On that night I had started on my way to becoming a Harlemite." But he follows this with a comment from his current vantage point: "I was going to become one of the most depraved parasitical hustlers among New York's eight million people."

On the train, Malcolm sells sandwiches, quickly realizing that "all you had to do was give white people a show and they'd buy anything you offered them. It was like popping your shoeshine rag." He uses his job to demonstrate his point that "white people are so obsessed with their own importance that they will pay liberally, even dearly, for the impression of being catered to and entertained." But as he grows more reckless and aggressive, "such an uncouth, wild young Negro," he creates tense situations with the customers and almost gets into a fight with a white soldier.

He divides his time between three places—Roxbury, Harlem, and the railroad: "At home in Roxbury, they would see me parading with Sophia, dressed in my wild zoot suits. Then I'd come to work, loud and wild and half-high on liquor or reefers, and I'd stay that way, jamming sandwiches at people until we got to New York." Eventually his aggressive performance gets him fired. Out of work, he visits family in Michigan, shocking them with his Harlem attire and "fire red" conk: "My conk and whole costume were so wild that I might have been taken as a man from Mars." Among the crowd in Michigan, he is seen practically as a celebrity and even signs autographs. Malcolm feels like he has achieved success: "I left Lansing shocked and rocked."

Back in Harlem, he is thrilled to get a job as a day waiter at Small's. The regulars like him, and he shows them respect: "Every day I listened raptly to customers who felt like talking, and it all added to my education. My ears soaked it up like sponges." He learns about the history of Harlem, about hustling, and the etiquette of the Harlem underworld: "I was thus schooled well, by experts in such hustles as the numbers, pimping, con games of many kinds, peddling dope and thievery of all sorts, including armed robbery."

In Chapters 6 and 7, Malcolm undergoes his next transformation, emerging as the hustler Detroit Red. These chapters vividly portray the tough side of the ghetto but also depict the strength of the black community. Malcolm describes the various characters he meets in Harlem, including the pimp Cadillac Drake and one of his prostitutes, Alabama Peach, a white woman, as well as "Fewclothes," a homeless man who Malcolm and the others at Small's provide with meals, serving him "as though he were a millionaire."

As Malcolm describes the ghetto, he also explains how white society helps to create and then profit from urban decay. Critic Maria Josefina Saldaña-Portillo attests that there are two central settings that Malcolm X describes as savage and uncivilized: "White America is the territory of the devil. Within the uncivilized space of white America, there is another uncivilized space, the ghetto. The ghetto is a wilderness within the wilderness: its violence, poverty, and crimes are the cynical and intended results of white barbarity" (p. 291). White society has oppressed blacks for centuries, from the days of slavery and continuing through segregation. By patronizing Harlem and demanding drugs or prostitutes, whites make it harder for the black inhabitants to rise above the conditions.

Malcolm points out the unrealized potential of his various friends. For example, Sammy the Pimp could have been a good businessman, and the gambler West Indian Archie, with his photographic memory and ability with math and computation, could have been successful in a legitimate line of work, had he been given an opportunity. Despite the struggles and the depth of their despair, Malcolm also points out the strong feeling of community, which later will fuel his views on black separatism:

Many times since, I have thought about it, and what it really meant. In one sense, we were huddled in there, bonded together in seeking security and warmth and comfort from each other, and we didn't know it. All of us—who might have probed space, or cured cancer, or built industries—were, instead, black victims of the white man's American social system.

To survive in the jungle, the ghetto, "almost everyone in Harlem needed some kind of hustle to survive, and needed to stay high in some way to forget what they had to *do* to survive." Malcolm moves into a rooming house run by prostitutes and continues to see Sophia whenever she comes to New York. Although Sophia marries a white man, she continues to see Malcolm while her husband is overseas serving in World War II. For Malcolm, her marriage "made no difference." He loses his job at Small's, after he refers an undercover military agent to a prostitute. With the help of Sammy the Pimp, he turns to selling drugs to New York jazz musicians. Malcolm smokes along with his customers, and "none of them stayed any more high than I did." Throughout Chapters 6 and 7, Malcolm dramatizes his downward spiral into crime, creating a dramatic tension and foreshadowing his eventual redemption. He describes his life then: "When you become an animal, a vulture, in the ghetto, as I had become, you enter a world of animals and vultures. It becomes truly the survival of only the fittest." Yet as critic El-Beshti points out, the readers also are to understand that "The hustling underworld, nevertheless, afforded Malcolm a sense of community and racial pride" (p. 364).

His drug-dealing business is a success until the local narcotics squad begins tailing him, and he must move to a new apartment each week to avoid being arrested on planted evidence. It is Sammy's idea for him to use his old railroad ID— this way, he can get away from the cops and "travel all over the East Coast selling reefers among my friends who were on tour with their bands." In 1943 the draft board summons Malcolm. By dressing outlandishly and telling the army psychologist that he wishes to lead southern blacks in an uprising to murder southern whites, he evades the draft.

In Chapter 7, "Hustler," Malcolm explains: "I was a true hustler—uneducated, unskilled at anything honorable, and I considered myself nervy and cunning enough to live by my wits, exploiting any prey that presented itself. I would risk just about anything." When his brother Reginald moves to Harlem, Malcolm gets him involved in the hustle of selling "cheap imperfect 'seconds'—shirts, underwear, cheap rings, watches, all kinds of quick-sale items," pretending the items are stolen. Malcolm pulls robberies and snorts cocaine, and in the evenings he hangs out at the Roxy and Paramount, where "I was known to almost every popular Negro musician around New York in 1944–1945."

He describes how whites would come up to Harlem after hours to go slumming: "Especially after nightclubs downtown closed, the taxis and black limousines would be driving uptown, bringing those white people who never could get enough of Negro *soul*." During this period, racial tensions escalate and conditions in Harlem worsen, leading to the night white police officers kill a black soldier at the Braddock Hotel, setting off a riot: "After the riot, things got very tight in Harlem." The police become more of an imposing presence, and fewer whites venture uptown. When the mayor shuts down the Savoy Ballroom, the Harlem community believes it is to put a stop to interracial dating.

Violence becomes a normal way of life for Malcolm, and he has a falling out with Sammy the Pimp, after Malcolm slaps Sammy's girlfriend and Sammy chases him with a gun. "I just couldn't forget that incident over Sammy's woman. I came to rely more and more upon my brother Reginald as the only one in my world I could completely trust."

For a while Malcolm works for a madam, "steering" white men from downtown to black prostitutes. He also imports bottles of liquor from Long Island for Hymie, a Jewish businessman: "Hymie really liked me and I liked him." However, Hymie mysteriously disappears after a scandal involving bootlegging.

During this time, Malcolm is constantly high on drugs and hanging out with his friends, including many famous people, such as Billie Holiday. He also gambles, playing the numbers more and more heavily; in Chapter 8, "Trapped," a conflict develops between West Indian Archie and Malcolm, when Archie accuses him of collecting winnings on a bet that he did not place. Malcolm insists he remembered correctly. Archie gives Malcolm a day to return the money, but Malcolm proceeds only to get high on drugs. The tension between Malcolm and Archie escalates when they run into each other at a bar; if Archie's friends had not stepped between them, they probably would have "shot it out in the street." Malcolm spends the rest of the night doing drugs: "The amount of dope I put into myself within the next several hours sounds inconceivable." The drama intensifies when he punches a young hustler and is almost stabbed in return. He is then being pursued by the hustler he punched, the police, West Indian Archie, and Italian racketeers who accuse him of robbing their craps game. Sammy the Pimp eventually contacts Malcolm's old friend Shorty, who arrives to take Malcolm back to Boston.

Chapter 9, "Caught," is the last chapter before Malcolm undergoes his most significant transformation up to that point. The chapter dramatizes Malcolm's downfall and depicts the depth to which he has sunk, juxtaposing this point in his life with the dramatic conversion he will undergo in prison. These years of crime are necessary for Malcolm's personal growth and for the development of his ideology and intellect.

Both Ella and Shorty are shocked by the way he has changed: "Ella couldn't believe how atheist, how uncouth I had become." Malcolm adds, "Every word I spoke was hip or profane. I would bet that my working vocabulary wasn't two hundred words," a detail that helps to contrast who he was at that point in time with the intellectually rigorous person he will become. Even Shorty is unnerved, not "prepared for how I lived and thought—like a predatory animal." Malcolm is still seeing Sophia, whose husband "never dreamed I existed." He treats Sophia badly, wondering why she sticks by him and gives him money, even when "I would feel evil and slap her around worse than ever."

In Boston, Malcolm quickly gains a reputation as someone who is wild and fearless, which he demonstrates during a poker game: "Looking back, I think I really was at least slightly out of my mind. I viewed narcotics as most people regard food. I wore my guns as today I wear my neckties." To make money for drugs, he starts pulling burglaries, recruiting Shorty, a local black Italian named Rudy, and Sophia and her sister. The two women scope out the white neighborhoods, since they will not arouse suspicion, then the men commit armed robbery, one of them driving the getaway car. Malcolm finds himself "spending money as though it were going out of style." Though he knows that a black detective who "had never been able to stand me, and it was mutual" is suspicious, Malcolm has grown too reckless to care: "I had gotten to the point where I was walking on my own coffin." One night when he is out, high on cocaine, he spots Sophia with a white man, a friend of her husband's, and Malcolm addresses her, blowing her cover. The man hunts for Malcolm later that night but then leaves his apartment without an altercation. Malcolm realizes that he is at the breaking point.

His life of crime ends when he drops off a stolen watch to a jewelry store to get a crystal replaced. When he returns to the store to pick it up, the police are waiting. Malcolm surrenders peacefully: "I didn't try to shoot [the cop]. And that saved my life." While the women receive low bail—"Their worst crime was their involvement with Negroes"—the bail for Shorty and Malcolm is set at $10,000 each. The details of his arrest and sentencing leave a strong impression on Malcolm, as he quickly realizes his "real" crime: "Nobody wanted to know anything at all about the robberies. All they could see was that we had taken the white man's women." Malcolm uses this personal example to illustrate how whites' racist fear of black men contaminates the various structures of society, including legal institutions: "Later, when I had learned the full truth about the white man, I reflected many times that the average burglary sentence for a first offender, as we all were, was about two years. But we weren't going to get the average—not for *our* crime."

5

Chapters 10 and 11 span the years that Malcolm spends in prison—a period of intellectual growth and religious upheaval. In prison, Malcolm develops his understanding of race, beginning to see all black people, and not just himself, as victims of racism and exploitation. This changing perception will influence the antiwhite rhetoric and militant black separatist views that he will come to embrace.

Malcolm and Shorty are each sentenced to ten years in prison, while the women receive one to five years. Malcolm, not yet twenty-one, is sent to Charlestown State Prison, where he is "physically miserable and as evil-tempered as a snake, being suddenly without drugs." He tries to get high in prison, first on nutmeg, then buys actual drugs from the prison guards: "I got reefers, Nembutal, and benzedrine." His first year at Charlestown is a blur of "semi-drugs, of cursing guards, throwing things out of my cell." For breaking rules, he is sent to solitary confinement where "I would pace for hours like a caged leopard, viciously cursing aloud to myself. And my favorite targets were the Bible and God." The other inmates nickname him Satan because "of my antireligious attitude." The beginning of this chapter works as a dramatic device, revealing just how much of a radical transformation he undergoes when he finds Allah.

Malcolm encounters one positive influence during his first year in prison, a confident, well-read older black prisoner, Bimbi, who commands the respect of both the guards and inmates. Bimbi "liked to talk about historical events and figures" and speaks on a wide range of subjects, including the author and naturalist Henry David Thoreau. Bimbi represents one of the many father figures who appear throughout Malcolm's life. In Boston, when he first arrived, Shorty served as Malcolm's teacher and guide, and now Bimbi assumes this role. Throughout the book, Malcolm gravitates to father figures that provide him with guidance and express confidence in him.

Under Bimbi's influence, Malcolm begins to think outside of his hustler's frame of mind. He takes advantage of the prison correspondence courses and the library, realizing, "the streets had erased everything I'd ever learned in school; I didn't know a verb from a house." He enrolls in a correspondence course in English, and after about a year, interested in word derivations, starts a course in Latin.

While in prison, Malcolm receives a letter from his brother Philbert, who was "forever joining something," saying that he had converted to the "'natural religion for the black man.'" Then a letter arrives from Reginald, who has also converted. He instructs Malcolm to stop smoking and eating pork but does not tell him why. Malcolm thinks it must be a way to "'get out of prison'" and does not yet realize this is one of the first steps toward becoming a Muslim.

Ella helps Malcolm get transferred to the Norfolk Prison Colony, an experimental rehabilitation jail, where "there were no bars, only walls—and within the walls, you had far more freedom. There was plenty of fresh air to breathe." At Norfolk the prisoners are encouraged to study. There is a debate team, a library with a diverse selection of books, and classes taught by instructors from Harvard and Boston universities.

Malcolm discovers that all of his siblings in Detroit and Chicago have converted to Islam. His brother Reginald visits and tells him about the Nation of Islam's spiritual leader, the Honorable Elijah Muhammad, and one of his central teachings, that "'The white man is the devil.'" At first Malcolm is troubled: "To say I was confused is an understatement." He has known kind white people, such as the Swerlins, and he asks his brother about "Hymie, the Jew, who had been so good to me," but his brother tells him there are no exceptions. As Malcolm begins to think of the other whites he has known in his life, such as the welfare workers who broke up his home, the teacher who discouraged him from becoming a lawyer, and the judge who sentenced him, the idea begins to make sense to him. He starts thinking in ways he never had before: "When Reginald left, he left me rocking with some of the first serious thoughts I had ever had in my life."

After Reginald's visit, Malcolm begins to receive at least two letters a day from his siblings in Detroit telling him more about the Nation of Islam. This religious sect began as a militant, separatist movement, an authoritarian religious organization with a very small following. Many of the views and doctrines reversed white racist beliefs. According to Elijah Muhammad, the original human race was black and lived peacefully in Africa under Allah in Mecca, until a mad scientist, Mr. Yacub, unleashed across Europe an evil white race that conspired to abuse nonwhites for six thousand years: "The devil white man cut these black people off from all knowledge of their own kind, and cut them off from any knowledge of their own language, religion, and past culture, until the black man in America was the earth's only race of people who had absolutely no knowledge of his true identity." Blacks were stolen from Africa, sold into slavery, and brainwashed—as whites forced them to adopt their names and religion. Elijah emphasizes that Christianity is the white man's religion, teaching black people to "worship an alien God having the same blond hair, pale skin, and blue eyes as the slave master," a religion that taught the black man "to hate everything black, including himself. It taught him that everything white was good, to be admired, respected, and loved."

Malcolm feels thunderstruck by these teachings and believes that his sins of the past have prepared him to accept these doctrines. The Afrocentric teachings that privilege black people and declare them to be superior appeal to him, as the critics Celeste Michelle Condit and John Louis Lucaites point out: "The founding myth of the Black Muslim faith legitimized and empowered the history and culture of Black society, and, upon encountering it, Malcolm converted almost immediately" (p. 295).

After his sister Hilda encourages him, Malcolm writes a letter to Elijah Muhammad and is surprised and moved when Elijah Muhammad writes back, instructing him to "have courage," and includes five dollars in the envelope. After that, Malcolm writes a letter a day to Elijah Muhammad expressing his devotion and also writes to his family and the "people I had known in the hustling world," to spread the word about the Nation of Islam. As Malcolm devotes himself to becoming a Muslim, he also experiences a tremendous intellectual growth, documented in Chapter 11, "Saved."

Malcolm soon feels frustrated by his limitations in expressing himself on the page. "It was because of my letters that I happened to stumble upon starting to acquire some kind of a homemade education," he explains. Though he has been reading regularly since Bimbi's initial encouragement, when Malcolm does not know the meaning of words, he skims over them. He then makes a radical decision: "I saw that the best thing I could do was get hold of a dictionary—to study, to learn some words."

Amazed by how many words are listed in the dictionary, Malcolm does not know where to begin:

Finally, just to start some kind of action, I began copying. In my slow, painstaking, ragged handwriting, I copied into my tablet everything printed on that first page, down to the punctuation marks. I believe it took me a day. Then, aloud, I read back, to myself, everything I'd written on the tablet. Over and over, aloud, to myself, I read my own handwriting.

He starts with the first word in the dictionary, *aardvark*, and slowly continues copying word by word, until he has filled an entire tablet with the As, then goes on to the Bs: "That was the way I started copying what eventually became the entire dictionary."

Malcolm immerses himself in books on a variety of subjects: linguistics, history, religion, biology, and literature. Now with his expanded vocabulary, when he picks up a book to read, he understands it, and this changes his life: "Anyone who has read a great deal can imagine the new world that opened. Let me tell you something: from then until I left that prison, in every free moment I had, if I was not reading in the library, I was reading on my bunk." He reads voraciously, staying up half the night to read by a crack of light that shines in from the hallway.

This chapter illustrates his rage and dogmatic views, which are both contrasted and fueled by his thirst for knowledge and his innately curious nature:

> I knew right there in prison that reading had changed forever the course of my life. As I see it today, the ability to read awoke inside me some long dormant craving to be mentally alive. I certainly wasn't seeking any degree, the way a college confers a status symbol upon its students. My homemade education gave me, with every additional book that I read, a little bit more sensitivity to the deafness, dumbness, and blindness that was afflicting the black race in America.

Reading becomes one of Malcolm's favorite ways to spend his time: "If I weren't out here every day battling the white man, I could spend the rest of my life reading, just satisfying my curiosity—because you can hardly mention anything I'm not curious about." But it is also a way for him to formulate his observations and ideas into a more coherent political philosophy. He develops a system of belief locating Africa as its center, finding his facts from respectable sources: "I took special pains to hunt in the library for books that would inform me on details about black history." He learns that the great early civilizations were African, as were the pharaohs and Aesop, the great Western storyteller. He becomes familiar with Black Nationalist thought and comes to understand the extent to which he had been brainwashed by the dominant culture.

When he is not reading, Malcolm seeks to convert fellow prisoners to the Nation of Islam. The prison's weekly debating program is his "baptism into public speaking." He immediately falls in love with it: "But I will tell you that, right there, in the prison, debating, speaking to a crowd, was as exhilarating to me as the discovery of knowledge through reading had been." He always finds a way to work race into his arguments, whether about Shakespeare or the military, and is pleased when he gets a white minister to admit that Jesus was not white, causing a stir of excitement in the prison. Malcolm now has discovered his purpose: "It was right there in prison that I made up my mind to devote the rest of my life to telling the white man about himself—or die."

He feels troubled when his brother Reginald begins to speak badly of Elijah: "It caught me totally unprepared. It threw me into a state of confusion." He learns that Reginald has been suspended from the Nation for "improper relations" with a secretary. Feeling confused, Malcolm writes a letter to Elijah, in an attempt to defend his brother. That night, he experiences a vision of a man visiting his prison cell and believes it to be a "pre-vision" of Master W.D. Fard, "the Messiah, the one whom Elijah Muhammad said had appointed him."

When Elijah sends a reply defending the Nation's position, Malcolm is convinced: "All of the influence that my brother had wielded over me was broken." Though Reginald continues to visit, when he speaks, Malcolm, "heard him coldly." Reginald eventually has a mental breakdown and enters an institution. For the first time, Malcolm feels a stronger bond to his faith than to his family.

6

In the spring of 1952, Malcolm is paroled from prison and released into the custody of his brother Wilfred in Detroit. Once freed, in Chapter 12, "Savior," his first purchases are a pair of eyeglasses (the late-night reading in prison gave him astigmatism), a suitcase, and a wristwatch: "I have thought, since, that without fully knowing it, I was preparing for what my life was about to become. Because those are three things I've used more than anything else." Malcolm is making a symbolic commitment to the beginning of his career as a religious and political authority. The watch symbolizes his obsession with efficiency; the suitcase represents his frequent travel and his devotion to his work and spreading the word; and the glasses symbolize his newfound clarity of vision on race in America. Now he is committed to bring this message to African Americans, ready to launch into a new life.

Malcolm appreciates the order of his brother's strict Muslim house and feels comforted by the rituals. When he attends services at Detroit Temple Number One, which at the time is a storefront located near hog-slaughtering pens, he feels welcomed by the congregation, and he appreciates the conservative dress, the respectful, warm salutations, and the solidarity and austerity. The highlight of his release from prison occurs when he visits Chicago's Temple Number Two to hear Elijah Muhammad speak. The man he'd written to every day in prison now stands at the front of the temple, flanked by guards, and Malcolm feels a deep respect for him: "The Messenger, compared to them, seemed fragile, almost tiny." When Elijah finishes his lecture, he calls Malcolm's name, and "[i]t was like an electrical shock. Not looking at me directly, he asked me to stand." Elijah explains to the members that Malcolm just got out prison, comparing him to the biblical figure Job and predicting that he will become one of his most devoted followers.

As a final symbolic act, Malcolm replaces his last name with "X" to represent the unknown African name he would have had if his ancestors had not been sold into slavery: "For me, my 'X' replaced the white slave master name of 'Little' which some blue-eyed devil named Little had imposed upon my paternal forebears." He begins to work for the Nation immediately, seeking to recruit new members: "in the Detroit ghetto bars, in the poolrooms, and on the corners, I found my poor, ignorant, brainwashed black brothers mostly too deaf, dumb, and blind, mentally, morally, and spiritually, to respond." At first he has little success, but after a few months, membership increases.

For income, Malcolm works various jobs, including at a furniture store with Wilfred and later at the Ford Motor Company. He begins to speak at temple meetings, gaining confidence as a public speaker: "my favorite subject was Christianity and the horrors of slavery." In the summer of 1953, he is humbled when he is named Detroit Temple Number One's assistant minister.

In Chapter 12, "Savior," Malcolm tells the personal history of Elijah Muhammad. Born in Georgia in 1897, Elijah, even as a child, felt a strong sense of pride and love for his race. In 1931, he met Wallace D. Fard, a peddler of silks and self-proclaimed prophet who converted Elijah to his version of Islam. When Fard disappeared in 1934, Elijah became head of the Nation. Threats from jealous rivals caused him to move frequently over a period of seven years, and he also spent time in prison, supposedly for draft evasion, although he was actually too old to serve in the military. In the 1940s, he reclaimed his position as the head of the Nation of Islam. Elijah's confidence in Malcolm instills in him an absolute devotion, and his love for and worship of Elijah foreshadows how this blind faith, which lasts nearly twelve years, will eventually threaten to topple his faith in Islam.

In Chapter 13, "Minster Malcolm X," Malcolm quits his job at Ford and begins extensive training, under the guidance of Elijah Muhammad, to become a minister. The two develop a close relationship like that of a father and son. Malcolm travels and speaks at temples, spreading the word and fully developing his rhetorical style. He is a charismatic, articulate, and persuasive speaker. When he goes to Boston to aid in the founding of a new temple, his sister Ella is amazed. She listens to him speak but does not convert: "She sat, staring, as though she couldn't believe it was me."

Early in the summer of 1954, Malcolm is deeply honored when Elijah appoints him to be the minister of Temple Seven in New York City, which at that time was a little storefront in Harlem. Malcolm seeks out his old crowd from the hustling days: "With my natural kinky red hair now close-cropped, in place of the old long-haired, lye-cooked conk they had always known on my head, I know I looked much different." His change in appearance and his clothing symbolize Malcolm's transformation into a religious and political leader. He sadly discovers that Sammy the Pimp is dead and that West Indian Archie is dying.

Every day in Harlem, Malcolm is out "fishing" for converts, tailoring his speeches to his given audience. His street smarts and his easy use of slang make him more persuasive to young urban blacks than many of his Christian competitors. His life as a hustler and his education in prison have helped him to understand the oppression of the ghetto. He empathizes with the depth of anger, alienation, and pain that often marked life there. Although many people gather to listen to him, few convert to Islam, which Malcolm believes has to do with the strict rules—no tobacco, alcohol, or drugs, no dancing, gambling, dating, movies, or sports—but also because they are too weighed down by social, economic, and political struggles to be moved. He begins to understand that for African Americans to be successful, they must be aggressive about helping one another.

At this point, the Nation of Islam has limited funds to work with, and Malcolm personally owns nothing except clothes, a watch, and a suitcase. The car he drives, and puts 30,000 miles on in five months, belongs to the Nation of Islam. Malcolm is instrumental in helping to establish more temples across the United States. Though the Nation of Islam is growing, "It just grew too slowly to suit me." His eagerness and blend of religion and politics reveal a difference between Malcolm, who is constantly traveling, proselytizing, and lecturing, and Elijah, who cautions Malcolm to be patient.

Malcolm is so devoted to the Nation that he expresses little interest in women. Since his conversion, he has been celibate and fully devoted to his work. For the majority of the autobiography, Malcolm reveals troubling gender politics— from his hustler days of abusing and prostituting women to his days as a minister, when he believes "women's true nature is to be weak." Most of his attitudes regarding women are misogynistic: "women were only tricky, deceitful, untrustworthy flesh." Though there is evidence that by the end of his life he rejected some of these sexist beliefs, there are no major changes expressed within the autobiography itself.

After he notices a woman at the temple, he begins thinking about marriage but does not act until he considers "how it would affect the Nation of Islam organization as a whole." He talks over his plans with Elijah and, after receiving his permission, abruptly proposes to Betty from a pay phone at a gas station: "I wasn't about to say any of that romance stuff that Hollywood and television had filled women's heads with. If I was going to do something, I was going to do it directly."

Betty and Malcolm eventually move to a seven-room house, financed by the Nation, in Queens, New York. Their first daughter, Attilah, is born in November 1958. Malcolm and Betty would have four daughters, while Malcolm was alive, and twin daughters after Malcolm's death. Though Betty does not become a central character in the book, readers understand her to be a major source of support for Malcolm, who admits, "I guess by now I will say I love Betty. She's the only woman I ever even thought about loving."

Malcolm is surprised and delighted when his sister Ella converts; "it had taken five years." The Nation receives more attention after one of its members is attacked by the police. Malcolm and fifty other men, part of the Fruit of Islam, an elite youth group, lead a mass demonstration, standing "in ranks-formation outside the police precinct house," demanding that the bleeding man be taken to the hospital. The police are "nervous and scared of the gathering crowd outside," especially as people in Harlem begin to join them: "Harlem's black people were long since sick and tired of police brutality. And they never had seen any organization of black men take a firm stand as we were." The incident makes front page of the *Amsterdam News*, "and for the first time the black man, woman, and child in the streets [were] discussing 'those Muslims.'"

7

The Nation of Islam begins to gain more publicity in Chapter 14, "Black Muslims." In 1959 *The Mike Wallace Show* produces a segment on the Muslims called "The Hate That Hate Produced," which is "edited tightly into a kaleidoscope of 'shocker' images." Professor C. Eric Lincoln publishes the book *The Black Muslims in America*. Malcolm resents the name "Black Muslims," but the media refuse to adopt a suitable replacement. He develops a love/hate relationship with the media, aggressively pursuing coverage as a platform to spread the words of Elijah Muhammad, yet also distrusting the press and television news reporters. After he buys a secondhand camera—"I don't know how many rolls of film I shot until I could take usable pictures"—he creates the Nation of Islam's own newspaper, *Muhammad Speaks*. This action reveals Malcolm's curiosity and eagerness to learn and, more significantly, shows his commitment to publicize the Nation and his belief in the power of the media.

Now that Black Muslims are in the public eye, their views cause controversy among whites and black civil rights leaders, who Malcolm becomes increasingly critical of, calling them "'integration'-mad Negroes" and "Uncle Toms." Unlike Martin Luther King, Jr., Malcolm X believes in segregation and shows little tolerance for King's peaceful tactics. As black civil rights leaders routinely criticize the Nation, Elijah at first advises Malcolm to be calm and not to respond because "one of the white man's tricks was keeping the black race divided and fighting against each other." After the verbal attacks become more frequent, though, he allows Malcolm to publicly vent his feelings.

Malcolm also espouses many of his beliefs about the "devil" white men to the white reporters, adding fuel to the fire: "I can remember those hot telephone sessions with those reporters as if it were yesterday. The reporters were angry. I was angry." As the Nation of Islam enters into America's consciousness through "hot, hot copy, both in the white and the black press," Malcolm rises as the most prevalent and persistent speaker for the Nation, participating in debates and appearing frequently on radio and television. He spends several hours each day on the phone and, increasingly, represents Elijah Muhammad on panels and lectures.

The Nation builds more temples and recruits more members, and by 1960 the organization is holding mass rallies, at which thousands show up to see and hear Elijah Muhammad: "America had never seen such fantastic all-black meetings!" At first, whites are barred from attending, "the first time the American black man had ever dreamed of such a thing." After several big rallies, the Nation begins to let in the white press, and, later, any white person can attend but must sit in a small separate section. As the Nation becomes more widely known, its members also attract the attentions of the FBI and police: "We were watched. Our telephones were tapped." The local police and FBI persistently question them, and black agents infiltrate the organization. Part of their interest stems from the fact that the Nation of Islam recruits many convicts.

By 1961 the Nation is flourishing, with new members, more money, and even greater publicity. As Elijah battles severe asthma, the Nation buys him a house in Arizona, where he spends most of the year, cutting back on his speaking engagements. With his worsening health and geographical distance, he gives more freedom to Malcolm: "He said that my guideline should be whatever I felt was wise—whatever was in the general good interests of our Nation of Islam." Malcolm is more interested in engaging in action for racial justice, whereas Elijah Muhammad prefers to stay out of politics. As Malcolm takes on a bigger role, Elijah warns him, "You will grow to be hated when you become well known. Because usually people get jealous of public figures." This foreshadows the tension between them, as Malcolm explains, "Nothing that Mr. Muhammad ever said to me was more prophetic."

In Chapter 15, "Icarus," Malcolm X continues to be known around the United States, speaking on radio and television and at colleges as well. At the same time, in 1963, the civil rights movement gains momentous power. As brutal images of southern white police officers using firehoses and dogs on African American children and demonstrators are broadcast across America, racial tensions increase, and many in the Nation are outraged and horrified. The assassination of NAACP field secretary Medgar Evers and the bombing of a black church in Alabama that claims the lives of four black girls in 1963 are turning points for the movement.

With Malcolm espousing his unwavering belief that black separatism is the only means to resist white oppression, he further severs himself from mainstream civil rights leaders, causing controversy and anger with his fiery statements against integration. He believes that African Americans need to separate from white society, to own their own businesses and patronize their own shops. He calls the March on Washington the "Farce on Washington." What he imagined as a "militant, unorganized, and leaderless" mass of African Americans is turned into something safe for and approved by whites: "What originally was planned to be an angry riptide, one English newspaper aptly described now as 'the gentle flood.'" Malcolm portrays himself as supremely self-confident and emotionally tough. He projects an image of being unbreakable and unbendable.

Civil rights leaders fight back, critiquing the Nation's racism and its militancy, as well as its unrealistic goals and lack of political involvement. As Condit and Lucaites point out, the Nation's idealistic insistence on a black nation did not sit well with civil rights leaders who were committed to changing the present-day situation in the United States: "Social and political policies conceived solely through a mythic vision are typically doomed to failure, and this was clearly the case here" (p. 297).

In spite of his controversial views, or perhaps because of them, the *New York Times* reports Malcolm X as the second most popular speaker on college campuses, right after Senator Barry Goldwater, who was running for president. A charismatic speaker, as evident in the spellbinding speeches he had made on street corners for the past decade, he now is a sought-after speaker at more than fifty universities, including Columbia, Yale, Harvard, and Brown. Malcolm admits, "Except for all-black audiences, I like the college audiences best," relishing the intellectual confrontations and enjoying the dynamics with the students, who are typically white. Elijah Muhammad, however, disapproves of the university lecture circuit and feels inferior to Malcolm's intelligence. Though Malcolm is obviously intellectually superior to Elijah, he completely surrenders himself to his spiritual leader and views him as a god, an attitude that reveals Malcolm's own naiveté and vulnerability.

8

In Chapter 16, "Out," the number of Nation members continues to grow, especially in New York, mostly due to Malcolm's efforts. He works tirelessly to promote Islam and spends as much time on the road as he did in New York:

I was crisscrossing North America sometimes as often as four times a week. Often, what sleep I got was caught in the jet planes. I was maintaining a marathon schedule of press, radio, television, and public-speaking commitments. The only way that I could keep up with my job for Mr. Muhammad was by flying with the wings that he had given me.

Though Malcolm feels pleased with the way Islam is growing, he also feels frustrated by the lack of direct action: "I thought privately that we should have amended, or relaxed, our general non-engagement policy. I felt that, wherever black people committed themselves, in the Little Rocks and the Birminghams and other places, militantly disciplined Muslims should also be there—for all the world to see, and respect, and discuss." Though Malcolm does not believe in integration, he is devoted to fighting for human rights for African Americans and committed to obtaining economic, educational, and political equality and justice. By expressing his views on the importance of political action, Malcolm further separates himself from his leader Elijah Muhammad, who does not want the Muslims to be associated or involved with politics.

As Malcolm X becomes increasingly popular and recognizable, his fame surpasses that of Elijah and Malcolm begins to hear jealous comments from others that he is trying to take over the Nation. Yet Malcolm maintains that he never wanted to be the star: "I always made it crystal clear that I was Mr. Muhammad's *representative*." By 1962 he begins to notice that he is rarely mentioned in *Muhammad Speaks*, the newspaper that he founded. Afraid that others in the Nation see him as someone who is trying to surpass Elijah, he begins to refuse high-profile interviews in order to reduce the jealousy.

At the last rally at which Elijah and Malcolm X appear together, in 1963, Elijah calls Malcolm his "most faithful hard-working minister. He will follow me until he dies." It is around this time that in his lectures Malcolm begins speaking less about the moral codes: "I taught social doctrine to Muslims, and current events, and politics. I stayed wholly off the subject of morality." The reason for this shift is because "my faith had been shaken in a way that I can never fully describe. For I had discovered Muslims had been betrayed by Elijah Muhammad himself." Malcolm claims that as far back as 1955 he had heard rumors about Elijah's adultery but never believed the whispered allegations could be true: "And so my mind simply refused to accept anything so grotesque as adultery mentioned in the same breath with Mr. Muhammad's name." Now Elijah Muhammad faces paternity suits from several of his secretaries; Malcolm can no longer see his spiritual leader as a god.

For their transgressions, these women are brought before the Nation of Islam courts and sentenced to one to five years of isolation, punishments meted out by Elijah himself. Malcolm's own brother had been turned out of the Nation for his conduct, something that plagues Malcolm with guilt. Hoping that the rumors are false, Malcolm talks to one of Elijah's sons and then contacts three of the former secretaries, who promise him the accusations are true. From them he also learns that "while [Elijah Muhammad] was praising me to my face, he was tearing me apart behind my back."

Malcolm is so distraught that he finally writes Elijah: "I desperately wanted to find some way—some kind of a bridge—over which I was certain the Nation of Islam could be saved from self-destruction." In April 1964 Malcolm visits Elijah at his home in Phoenix and tells him what is on his mind. Instead of taking responsibility or admitting to his guilt, Elijah explains that his affairs are all part of a larger prophecy.

Malcolm fears that reporters will ask him about the rumors: "I felt like a total fool, out there every day preaching, and apparently not knowing what was going on right under my nose." Others notice that he is tired and under great strain, including white reporters, who express their sympathy: "Since I had been a Muslim this was the first time any white people really got to me in a personal way. I could tell that some of them were really honest and sincere." With this statement, Malcolm further distances himself from Elijah Muhammad—perhaps he is already recognizing that not all whites are categorically evil, as members of the Nation had represented them to be. With one white reporter, Malcolm engages in a full discussion, the "first time since I became a Muslim that I had ever talked with any white man at any length about anything except the Nation of Islam and the American black man's struggle today." The two men talk for two hours about "archaeology, history, and religion. It was *so* pleasant."

Relations between Malcolm and the Nation worsen when President John F. Kennedy is assassinated on November 22, 1963. Elijah instructs all of his ministers to respond to the media the same way: "Every minister was ordered to make no remarks at all concerning the assassination. Mr. Muhammad instructed that if pressed for comment, we should say: 'No comment,'" but Malcolm defies Elijah's order when he gives a speech in New York titled "God's Judgment of White America" and refers to the JFK assassination as a case of "the chickens coming home to roost," implying that the murder was understandable. The controversial statement makes headlines. As punishment, and to distance the Nation from Malcolm, Elijah silences him for ninety days. Humiliated, Malcolm accepts the punishment but privately believes that the real reason he is being silenced is because he would not keep quiet about Elijah's transgressions. Malcolm believes that his own accomplishments—expanding Nation membership and becoming a leading spokesman for the race problem in the United States—had threatened Elijah Muhammad. The silencing is an excuse to finally cast him off, as he believes the Nation had been planning to do for some time. "It makes me feel weary to think of it all now," he explains.

Then one of Malcolm's assistants confesses that the Nation has ordered him to kill Malcolm, and Malcolm believes that Elijah is behind it: "As any official in the Nation of Islam would instantly have known, any death-talk for me could have been approved of—if not actually initiated—by only one man." Malcolm is devastated: "My head felt like it was bleeding inside. I felt like my brain was damaged." To escape the turmoil and threat of violence, he accepts an invitation from the heavyweight boxer Cassius Clay for Malcolm and his family to stay in Florida. When Clay, a Muslim, wins the heavyweight championship, he changes his name to Muhammad Ali and becomes a hero to Muslims around the world. While in Florida, Malcolm tries to relax, but it is difficult: "But I could not yet let myself psychologically face what I knew: that already the Nation of Islam and I were physically divorced." He is deeply shocked by Elijah's fall from grace, but even more distraught by his betrayal: "I could conceive death. I couldn't conceive betrayal."

Malcolm decides to break off on his own and continue to serve the political and economic interests of African Americans. Using his popularity and celebrity status, he founds a new organization, Muslim Mosque, Inc., in Harlem, which will be more active in its pursuit of black political and economic independence. Some members "announced their break from the Nation of Islam to come with me." But before the organization really gets going, Malcolm feels it is time to make a pilgrimage to the Islamic holy city of Mecca. The betrayal of Elijah Muhammad, whom he had trusted absolutely, has shattered his faith, preparing him for the significant transformation that he undergoes in Chapter 17, "Mecca."

9

Cut off from his sole source of income, Malcolm asks for help from Ella, who has also withdrawn from the Nation. She agrees to finance his pilgrimage to Mecca, and Malcolm expresses his gratitude: "She had played a very significant role in my life. No other woman ever was strong enough to point me in directions." When Malcolm applies for a hajj visa, he learns that his status as a Muslim must be approved by Mahmoud Youssef Shawarbi, a Muslim United Nations adviser, who provides Malcolm with contacts in Saudi Arabia.

The pilgrimage to Mecca, the holy city in Saudi Arabia, known as the hajj, is a religious obligation that every orthodox Muslim attempts to fulfill at least once in his or her lifetime. Throughout Malcolm's twelve years as a minister for Elijah, when eastern Muslims had accused him of not understanding "true Islam," Malcolm always grew defensive: "Automatically, as a follower of Elijah Muhammad, I had bridled whenever this was said. But in the privacy of my own thoughts after several of these experiences, I did question myself: if one was sincere in professing a religion, why should he balk at broadening his knowledge of that religion?" His deep disappointment in Elijah has created a profound spiritual crisis, prompting his journey to Mecca and a search for truth.

When he lands in Cairo, Egypt, he is surprised by what he sees:

> Throngs of people, obviously Muslims from everywhere, bound on the pilgrimage, were hugging and embracing. They were of all complexions, the whole atmosphere was of warmth and friendliness. The feeling hit me that there really wasn't any color problem here. The effect was as though I had just stepped out of a prison.

This marks the beginning of Malcolm's radical transformation. On the next leg of the trip, to Jeddah, Saudi Arabia, he notices that everyone is dressed the same, in towels and sandals, and convinces himself that there is no division along class or racial lines. He provides many images of integration throughout the chapter: "Packed in the plane were white, black, brown, red, and yellow people, blue eyes and blond hair, and my kinky red hair—all together, brothers! All honoring the same God Allah, all in turn giving equal honor to each other."

Malcolm cannot go on to Mecca until he is approved by the Muslim high court: "It was absolute that no non-Muslim could enter Mecca." He waits at the crowded airport, reflecting on the various languages, races, and customs of the Muslims around him. Following the example of others, he learns to pray, a physically difficult task: "Imagine, being a Muslim minister . . . and not knowing the prayer ritual." Malcolm feels ashamed of how little he knows about Muslim traditions. The prayers are in Arabic, which he cannot speak. He also feels uncomfortable with the eating customs. Though people offer him food, "The trouble was, I have to admit it, at that point I didn't know if I could go for their manner of eating. Everything was in one pot on the dining room rug, and I saw them just fall right in, using their hands."

Malcolm calls Omar Azzam, a friend of Shawarbi's, and he meets him at the airport. Azzam's father, Dr. Abd ir-Rahman Azzam, is an intellectual and Arab diplomat who vacates his suite at the Jeddah Palace Hotel for Malcolm, who is greatly impressed by the hospitality: "I had never seen these men before in my life, and they treated me so good!" Dr. Azzam's white complexion inspires Malcolm to think more about race, and, perhaps naively, he decides that Muslim countries do not have racial problems: "But in the Muslim world, I had seen that men with white complexions were more genuinely brotherly than anyone else had ever been."

After Malcolm is deemed qualified to journey to Mecca, he arrives in a specially ordered car lent by Saudi Arabia's Prince Faisal himself. He describes his sense of wonder at Mecca: "The *brotherhood!* The people of all races, colors, from all over the world coming together as *one!* It has proved to me the power of the One God." At the end of his hajj, Malcolm writes a letter to his newly formed mosque in the United States and the press, expressing his new perspective on the racial problems there. "Even I was myself astounded. But there was precedent in my life for this letter. My whole life had been a chronology of—*changes.*"

Because he has met whites who seem to be untainted by racism, he can no longer believe that all whites espouse racial hatred. The color blindness he observes inspires him to consider some kind of racial integration, which he had previously deplored. He signs the letter "El-Hajj Malik El-Shabazz," which becomes his official name, representing his newfound self, though the world continues to refer to him as Malcolm X.

The "Muslim from America" causes excitement as he travels around Mecca, embracing what before had made him uncomfortable: "My hands now readily plucked up food from a common dish shared with bother Muslims; I was drinking without hesitation from the same glass as others; I was washing from the same little pitcher of water; and sleeping with eight or ten others on a mat in the open." While in Mecca, Malcolm speaks to others about racism in his native land. He learns that leaders and intellectuals of nonwhite nations are greatly interested in the plight of American blacks. The experience at Mecca leaves him forever changed: "A part of me, I left behind in the Holy City of Mecca. And, in turn, I took away with me—forever—a part of Mecca."

In Chapter 18, "El-Hajj Malik El-Shabazz," Malcolm flies to Lebanon, Ghana, Liberia, Senegal, and Morocco, meeting with many leaders and intellectuals of nonwhite countries, exposure that greatly influences his new political outlook. When he returns to the United States, more than fifty photographers and reporters are waiting for him at John F. Kennedy International Airport in New York City. They besiege him with questions and imply a link between him and race riots exploding around the country. Malcolm feels frustrated that the press fails to acknowledge his new outlook: "I knew I was back in America again, hearing the subjective, scapegoat-seeking questions of the white man."

In the last chapter, "1965," Malcolm, "the angriest Negro in America," tries to convey that he is "now attempting to teach Negroes a new direction" and to clarify his new position on whites, but "the white reporters kept wanting me linked with that word 'violence.'" In Harlem, he holds meetings for a new group, the Organization for Afro-American Unity, a non-religious assembly founded with the intent of uniting African Americans to fight for the attainment of human rights. The group emphasizes inclusiveness of people of any faith, though excludes whites from membership.

In the last year of his life, Malcolm returns to Africa and the Middle East to meet with world leaders, which helps him locate the plight of African Americans in an international context. As his political vision becomes more sophisticated, he makes fundamental links between racism, colonialism, and economic exploitation. He articulates a new vision for black Americans, to see themselves as one of a number of nonwhite minorities seeking justice:

> Malcolm X's new vision, born of his separation from Elijah Muhammad was truly revolutionary, in the sense that it established the basis for a whole new way

of thinking and talking about the relationship between Blacks and Whites. It was thus a revolution of identity, rather than a violent attempt to overthrow the prevailing social and political structures. (Condit, Lucaites, 302).

Malcolm has also fine-tuned his beliefs that "the white man is *not* inherently evil, but America's racist society influences him to act evilly." Though still militant, he displays more willingness to work with other civil rights groups.

Despite the many interviews and lectures, he encounters trouble building the new Black Nationalist organization, "my old so-called 'Black Muslim' image, kept blocking me. I was trying to gradually reshape that image." He recalls a young white woman who once came to the Nation's restaurant in Harlem, asking what she could do to help, and he had told her, "Nothing." Now he says, "I regret that I told her that. . . ." This admission is a strong avowal of Malcolm's profound change. He attests, "My friends today are black, brown, red, yellow, and *white!*" In his final conversion, Malcolm is drawn to a more utopian vision of a multicultural global community.

Malcolm knows that his life is vulnerable and predicts he will die a violent death, doubting that he will live to see the publication of the autobiography. Malcolm expresses that his greatest personal regret is that he does not have an academic education. He believes that he would have been a lawyer, as "I have always loved verbal battle, and challenge," and claims that if he had more time, "I would just like to *study*. I mean ranging study, because I have a wide-open mind."

10

In the epilogue, Alex Haley provides more information about the process of writing the book and traces the last two years of Malcolm's life, focusing on the days leading up to his death and its aftermath. Author John Wideman attests, "The Epilogue becomes an eloquent extension of the *Autobiography*, a gripping, dramatically structured fugue that impels the reader toward the climax of assassination, the inevitable slow shock of recognition afterward as the world assesses the loss of Malcolm" (p. 105).

The epilogue reminds readers that the book is not a traditional autobiography—for the first time we hear Haley providing us with his own point of view and personal thoughts.

Haley takes us behind the scenes, describing the interview sessions with Malcolm and allowing a more intimate view. At first, Haley almost gives up on the project because Malcolm refuses to reveal anything personal. But then Haley notices that while Malcolm is talking, he scribbles notes on napkins or scraps of paper that he sometimes leaves behind. After reading them, Haley discovers that these notes reveal more of Malcolm's personal ideas and unique thoughts. When Malcolm finally begins to open up about his mother and more personal aspects of his life, Haley begins to build a foundation for the book.

The epilogue sheds more light on Malcolm's complexity, contradictions, and vulnerability. Haley also touches on a lighter side of Malcolm. Though his mood usually remains grim when telling childhood stories, when he tells Haley about arriving in Boston, he laughs, recalling how out of place he looked. Then, in describing the lindy-hops, Malcolm becomes surprisingly animated: "One night, suddenly, wildly, he jumped up from his chair and, incredibly, the fearsome black demagogue was scat-singing and popping his fingers, 're-bop-de-bop-blap-blam—' and then grabbing a vertical pipe with one hand (as the girl partner) he went jubilantly lindy-hopping around, his coattail and the long legs and the big feet flying as they had in those Harlem days."

Haley also provides more insight into Malcolm's personal and political views. Even while he is espousing antiwhite rhetoric, Haley observes, "I saw Malcolm X too many times exhilarated in after-lecture give-and-take with predominately white student bodies at colleges and universities to ever believe that he nurtured at his core any blanket white-hatred." He also believed that Malcolm felt a "reluctant admiration of Dr. Martin Luther King." Haley spends time with Malcolm in Harlem and witnesses firsthand how happy he is when he goes on his "little daily rounds," grinning and conversing with anyone on the street. These are the people he is fighting for, and they consider him a hero.

When they start the project, both Malcolm and Haley assume the book will be a story of his conversion to the Nation of Islam and rise to become a minister for Elijah Muhammad. But then Malcolm experiences a major upheaval and breaks with Elijah Muhammad. After he returns from Mecca, he is a changed man. Haley worries that now Malcolm will want to rewrite the bulk of the narrative, and, indeed, when Haley sends him a few early chapters that focus on his close relationship with Elijah, the pages are returned covered in red ink. Haley convinces Malcolm that he cannot change the past: "I stressed that if those chapters contained such telegraphing to readers of what would lie ahead, then the book would automatically be robbed of some of its building suspense and drama."

Malcolm decides Haley is right and lets the chapters stand as they are, seeming to understand that his life has been a series of changes and that he cannot go back and revise past experiences. He can only look ahead and try to make sense of his new and changing views. He professes to Haley, "I hope the book is proceeding rapidly, for events concerning my life happen so swiftly, much of what has already been written can easily be outdated from month to month. In life, nothing is permanent; not even life itself." Critic Paul Eakin argues, "Malcolm X's final knowledge of the incompleteness of the self is what gives the last pages of the *Autobiography* together with the 'Epilogue' their remarkable power: the vision of a man whose swiftly unfolding career has outstripped the possibilities of the traditional autobiography he had meant to write."

Haley describes how tense Malcolm is during the days before his death and the violence leading up to that day. On February 14, 1965, Malcolm's house is firebombed. Although he and his wife and four daughters escape unharmed, the house is destroyed. Then, a week later, on February 21, at Harlem's Audubon Ballroom, three audience members rush the stage with guns and kill Malcolm X. Police arrest three suspects, allegedly Black Muslims, but controversy continues today, with suspicions persisting that larger forces were potentially behind the assassination.

During his lifetime, Malcolm X was one of the most admired and hated men in the United States. Decades after his death, his name continues to provoke many different emotions. The dramatic changes in Malcolm's life reveal his thirst for knowledge and quest for truth. Haley considers him to be one of the "most engaging personalities I had ever met." Malcolm X's reputation and influence as a black political activist and leader have continued to grow over the years, as the *Autobiography* still resonates with readers today.

Works Cited

Condit, Celeste Michelle and John Louis Lucaites, "Malcolm X and the Limits of the Rhetoric of Revolutionary Dissent," *Journal of Black Studies* 23, no. 3 (March 1993): pp. 291–313.

Demarest, Jr., David P., "*The Autobiography of Malcolm X*: Beyond Didacticism," *CLA Journal* 16, no. 2 (December 1972): pp. 179–187.

Eakin, Paul John, "Malcolm X and the Limits of Autobiography," *Criticism* 18 (1976): pp. 230–42. Reprinted in *African American Autobiography*. Englewood Cliffs, NJ: Prentice Hall, 1993: pp. 151–161.

El-Beshti, Bashir M. "The Semiotics of Salvation: Malcolm X and the Autobiographical Self," *The Journal of Negro History* 82, no. 4 (Autumn 1997): pp. 359–367.

Saldaña-Portillo, Maria Josefina, "Consuming Malcolm X: Prophecy and Performative Masculinity," *NOVEL* 30, no. 3 (Spring 1997): pp. 289–308.

Wideman, John Edgar, "Malcolm X: The Art of Autobiography." In *Malcolm X: In Our Own Image*. Joe Wood, ed. New York: St. Martin's Press, 1992: pp. 101–116.

▰ Critical Views

David P. Demarest, Jr. on Dual Authorship and the Book's Undogmatic Tone

Clearly *The Autobiography*'s literary effectiveness is enhanced by some of its didactic aspects—its carefully symmetrical structure, for instance. Beginning at the beginning, Malcolm narrates his childhood and his teenage life of crime. Finally in prison, feeling that he has become Satan incarnate, he undergoes his first conversion, to Elijah Muhammad's religion. The chapter titled "Saved" is right at mid-point in the book— pages 169 through 190 in a total that runs to 382. After chronicling his activities in the Nation of Islam and his gradual estrangement from Elijah, Malcolm ends with his trip to Mecca and Africa and his conversion to a larger, more inter-racial faith. Such a schematic pattern might be expected of a didactic autobiographer who sees his life as moral exemplum and who seeks converts through advertisement of the road to wisdom that has been opened to him. Undeniably, *The Autobiography* gains a good deal of strength from the balanced clarity of this overall structure.

Further, this conversion pattern lends strength to the book . . . because it evokes the tradition of spiritual autobiographies and wayfarings that runs deep through Christian literature. The stay in prison, as metaphor for man's fallible nature or unregenerate state, recalls Boethius and, more closely, *Grace Abounding to the Chief of Sinners*. Less literally, the prison episode suggests the adventures of another wayfarer, Robinson Crusoe, whose island imprisonment served, like Malcolm's legal detention, as stimulus to self-effort, self-education and conversion. Malcolm's procedure of learning language by copying the dictionary word by word and then studying the words of Elijah Muhammad is specifically reminiscent of the self-help faith of Robinson Crusoe's bibliolatry; it also recalls the scheduled self-improvements of the young Benjamin Franklin. Echoes of *Pilgrim's Progress* are found in the clean-living zeal, the puritanical quality of the Black Muslims emphasized by Malcolm. Literarily, *Pilgrim's Progress* is evoked by the journey to Mecca, the holy city, but it is also there in the early description of Harlem, which Malcolm presents as an entrapping Vanity Fair. When Malcolm calls the roll of the street names of the hustlers he knew, an allegorized world springs to life—The Four Horsemen (black cops who worked Sugar Hill); Cadillac Drake ("the world's most unlikely pimp"); Sammy the Pimp; Alabama Peach (a white prostitute who worked for Sammy); Dollarbill (another pimp who liked to flash his "Kansas City roll"); Fewclothes (a pickpocket); Jumpsteady (a burglar) (see pp. 88–90). Like Bunyan's, Malcolm's world is alive with identifying tags of meaning: every name signals a story—some adjustment to the hellish pressures of Harlem. . . .

> The world's most unlikely pimp was "Cadillac" Drake. He was shiny baldheaded, built like a football; he used to call his huge belly "the chippies' playground." Cadillac had a string of about a dozen of the stringiest, scrawniest, black and white street prostitutes in Harlem. Afternoons around the bar, the old-timers who knew Cadillac well enough would tease him about how women who looked like his made enough to feed themselves, let alone him. He'd roar with laughter right along with us; I can hear him now, "Bad-looking women work harder." (p. 88)

This paragraph—chosen almost at random—is perfectly typical of the style attributed to Malcolm by *The Autobiography*. It illustrates the simple and, above all, concrete vocabulary, and it shows the unelaborate sentence pattern that underlines the clarity and directness of Malcolm's voice. Also typical is the moralizing structure of the paragraph. The first sentence, neatly and explicitly, is the topic sentence; the last sentence lets Cadillac draw the moral. But the moralizing has a complex effect because its end is comic, and the reader warms to Malcolm as he senses a moralizer who can laugh at the conventions of moral-drawing.

Almost all the chapters, as well as the smaller episodes, end with exhortation and advice. Malcolm comments, for instance, about his decision to leave Michigan and go to Boston: "All praise is due to Allah that I went to Boston when I did. If I hadn't, I'd probably still be a brainwashed black Christian." (p. 38) After his first "conking" he concludes:

> I'm speaking from personal experience when I say of any black man who conks today, or any white-wigged black woman, that if they give the brains in their heads just half as much attention as they do their hair, they would be a thousand times better off. (p. 55)

Most of such moralizing is aimed at blacks—whether about conking, hustling, the numbers rackets, or about religious and political attitudes. But Malcolm calls for something larger than such specifics—self-awareness, self-criticism, and, often, the concomitant ability to laugh at oneself. Thus Malcolm can describe his zoot-suited elegance as a teenager and a visit back home to Michigan this way:

> ... I'd go through that Grand Central Station rush-hour crowd, and many white people simply stopped in their tracks to watch me pass. The drape and the cut of a zoot suit showed to the best advantage if you were tall—and I was over six feet. My conk was fire-red. I was really a clown, but my ignorance made me think I was "sharp." My knob-toed, orange-colored "kick-up" shoes were nothing but Florsheims, the ghetto's Cadillac of shoes in those days. ... (p. 78) My conk and whole costume were so wild that I might have been taken as a man from Mars. I caused a minor automobile collision; one driver stopped to gape at me, and the driver behind bumped into him. My appearance staggered the older boys I had once envied; I'd stick out my hand, saying "Skin me, daddy-o!" (p. 79) ....

... One might expect that a preacher (as Malcolm was) who wrote his autobiography in order to persuade and convert his readers would maintain a tone of voice that supported his didactic maxims. Everything should serve the purpose of conversion. Malcolm's voice—as in the examples above—is far more flexible. From his post-conversion perspective, Malcolm must look back at Small's bar in Harlem as a meeting place of ill-spent, misdirected lives, and he must lecture his black brothers to extricate themselves. But in his descriptions the world of the rackets and the hustlers—like his teenage zoot-suiting—comes brilliantly, even lovingly, to life. Malcolm relives it all in retrospect, not for a moment falling into the moralizer's trap of turning what he condemns into clay pigeons. A fine example of his ability to avoid the rigidities of didacticism is his description of dancing:

> If you've ever lindy-hopped, you'll know what I'm talking about. With most girls, you kind of work opposite them, circling, sidestepping, leading. Whichever arm you lead with is half-bent out there, your hands are giving that little push, that little push, touching her waist, her shoulders, her arms. She's in, out, turning, whirling, wherever you guide her. With poor partners, you feel their weight. They're slow and heavy. But with really good partners, all you need is just the push-pull suggestion. They guide effortlessly, even off the floor and into the air, and your little solo maneuver is done on the floor before they land, when they join you, whirling, right in step. (p. 63)

It is still an instructor's voice talking, but coming from a religious convert who is bent, overall, on showing his dance-hall experiences as the corrupt follies of ignorant youth, the teacher's voice is startlingly vivid with remembered pleasure. Malcolm's relish for the verve of some of his early life may technically point him toward contradiction with some of his preachments. But more significantly, in violating the demands of a strict, narrow logic, Malcolm's attitude reveals a more complex, even a more tolerant personality than one might expect.

It is unrealistic to talk long about *The Autobiography*'s undogmatic tone without speculating on how the book's double authorship (Malcolm-to-Alex Haley) may have been a determinant. One is tempted to feel that had the book been entirely Malcolm's, or had he lived and possibly forced certain revisions, the book would have revealed less of Malcolm than it now does. At least it probably would have been more dogmatic, cut more rigidly to the pattern of Malcolm's latest position. That Malcolm—the one that might have emerged from a book entirely controlled by Malcolm—would have revealed one true side of the real man, but it might have suppressed the qualities of openness and growth that Haley, as outside observer, could appreciate. As it stands, *The Autobiography* may avoid the problems of both the autobiographer's lack of objectivity and the biographer's limited knowledge.

Haley's comments in the Epilogue make it clear that Malcolm felt drawn by the spiritual autobiographer's temptation to adjust events to fit updated moral positions. Malcolm's personal feud with the Black Muslims in the last year of his life and his attempt to define for himself a more international position might well have led him to revise *The Autobiography* into a running attack on Elijah Muhammad. Alex Haley recounts how Malcolm's shifted attitude affected his literary judgment:

> . . . I sent Malcolm X some rough chapters to read. I was appalled when they were soon returned, red-inked in many places where he had told of his almost father-and-son relationship with Elijah Muhammad. Telephoning Malcolm X, I reminded him of his previous decision, and I stressed that if those chapters contained such telegraphing to the readers of what would lie ahead, then the book would automatically be robbed of some of its building suspense and drama. Malcolm X said, gruffly, "Whose book is this?" I told him "Yours, of course," and that I only made the suggestion in my position as a writer. He said that he would have to think about it. I was heart-sick at the prospect that he might want to re-edit the entire book into a polemic against Elijah Muhammad. But late that night, Malcolm X telephoned. "I'm sorry. You're

right. I was upset about something. Forget what I wanted changed, let what you already had stand." I never again gave him chapters to read unless I was with him. (p. 414)

In such fashion, the double authorship of *The Autobiography* checked Malcolm's tendencies to make the book too overtly polemic.

It is again a matter of speculation how differently Malcolm, left to his own devices, might have been tempted to treat the doctrinal tenets of the Nation of Islam that *The Autobiography* explains during and after the prison conversion. Either extreme might be expected in the didactic self-advertisement of the spiritual autobiography—either the unqualified affirmation of the new convert to the Nation of Islam, or a retrospective critical commentary—if not contempt—from the final convert to another creed. But Malcolm—perhaps checked by Haley—goes to neither extreme. A tone of qualified assent, for example, is given to the Muslim tenet that the white man is the devil. In his introductory comments, M. S. Handler states that what was "most disconcerting in our talk was Malcolm's belief in Elijah Muhammad's history of the origins of man, and in a genetic theory devised to prove the superiority of black over white—a theory stunning to me in its absurdity." (p. xi) But it is hard to know whether Malcolm accepted this theory literally. In the context of the autobiography, the theory is not fanatically supported—or attacked—but is presented rather as a useful metaphor, true in its expression of black superiority. The story is introduced at key points by "Elijah Muhammad teaches," and Malcolm expresses his initial incredulity at the story's details. (see pp. 164–168) What emerges in the tone of Malcolm's account is the belief in and retrospective regard for the truth of intention in Elijah's mythology—not that it need be literally true, but that it calculated truly the radical revision of race perspective needed to cope with the American problem. And what further emerges in Malcolm's tone is his refusal to be caught simplistically in dogma, his openness to revisions of his own.

The specific slogan that the white man is the devil is also handled with more qualification than one might expect.

Malcolm records his first hesitations of belief, remembering how his consent balked at Hymie, the Jewish bootlegger he'd once worked for. (p. 159) And then after his conversion, he explains the rationale and effect of the slogan.

> I always had to be careful. I never knew when some brain-washed black imp, some dyed-in-the-wool Uncle Tom, would nod at me and then go running to tell the white man. When one was ripe—and I could tell—then away from the rest, I'd drop it on him, what Mr. Muhammad taught: "The white man is the devil." That would shock many of them—until they started thinking about it. . . .
>
> You tell that to any Negro. Except for those relatively few "integration"-mad so-called "intellectuals," and those black men who are otherwise fat, happy, and deaf, dumb, and blinded, with their crumbs from the white man's rich table, you have struck a nerve center in the American black man. He may take a day to react, a month, a year; he may never respond, openly; but of one thing you can be sure—when he thinks about his own life, he is going to see where to him, personally, the white man sure has acted like a devil. (pp. 182–3)

The frankness with which Malcolm explains this slogan as a rhetorical device and apt metaphor again underscores his undogmatic sophistication. (A story told by Haley in the Epilogue suggests that even before his break with Elijah, Malcolm would not be trapped in belief in the literal truth of Elijah's doctrine: "The first time I ever heard Malcolm X speak of Handler, whom he had recently met, he began, 'I was talking with this devil—' and abruptly he cut himself off in obvious embarrassment. 'It's a reporter named Handler, from the *Times*—' he resumed."—p. 400). . . .

. . . But again the pattern of *The Autobiography* varies from what one might expect—a climatic summation of true values arrived at in the end. The apparent climax to Malcolm's book is in the two penultimate chapters, the journeys to Mecca and Africa as symbolic capstones to the twin religious and political thrusts of Malcolm's career. The last chapter, titled "1965," tends to be anticlimactic, to eddy into fragments—as though Malcolm does not quite know how or where to move next. Such, indeed, is the note sounded at the chapter's start: "I must be honest. Negroes—Afro-Americans—showed no inclination to rush to the United Nations and demand justice for themselves here in America." (p. 364) Haley's epilogue, which is integral to completing the chronology of Malcolm's life, emphasizes the false starts, the indecisions, the groping of Malcolm's last days. In one sense, the ending of *The Autobiography* is thus weak. The book does not end—as a didactic spiritual autobiographer might like it to and insist that it did—at the symbolic high-point. But again this variation from neat structure, if momentarily a letdown, actually has a positive effect—at least for the reader interested in the general human theme of the book. The ending enforces the questing nature of Malcolm's personality, making it seem too big to be summed up. Malcolm's growth has not stopped with Mecca and Africa but seems instead to be beginning anew on another expanding cycle.

PAUL JOHN EAKIN ON THE LIMITS OF AUTOBIOGRAPHY

Before we consider the *Autobiography* from the vantage point of the man who was becoming "El-Hajj Malik El-Shabazz" (Chapter 18), let us look at the *Autobiography* as it was originally conceived by the man whose first conversion in prison had transformed him from "Satan" (Chapter 10) to "Minister Malcolm X" (Chapter 13). This is, of course, the way we do look at the *Autobiography* when we begin to read it for the first time, especially if we are relatively unfamiliar with the life of Malcolm X.

The Malcolm X of these years was firmly in command of the shape of his life, tracing his sense of this shape to the pivotal and structuring illumination of conversion itself.[6] At this point his understanding of the design of his experience, especially his baffled fascination with the radical discontinuity between the old Adam and the new, closely parallels the state of St. Augustine, Jonathan Edwards, and many another sinner touched by gracious affections, so much so that the student of spiritual autobiography is likely to feel himself at home on familiar ground:

> For evil to bend its knees, admitting its guilt, to implore the forgiveness of God, is the hardest thing in the world. . . . When finally I was able to make myself stay down—I didn't know what to say to Allah. . . . I still marvel at how swiftly my previous life's thinking pattern slid away from me, like snow off a roof. It is as though someone else I knew of had lived by hustling and crime. I would be startled to catch myself thinking in a remote way of my earlier self as another person. (170)

If we consider Malcolm X's account of his life up to the time of his break with Elijah Muhammad (in Chapter 16, appropriately entitled "Out"), what we have in fact is a story that falls rather neatly into two sections roughly equal in length, devoted respectively to his former life as a sinner (Chapters 3–9) and to his present life as one of Elijah Muhammad's ministers (Chapters 10–15). This two-part structure is punctuated by two decisive experiences: his repudiation of the white world of his youth in Mason, Michigan, and his conversion to Islam in prison at Norfolk, Massachusetts.

Malcolm X describes the "first major turning point of my life" (35) at the end of the second chapter, his realization that in white society he was not free "to become whatever I wanted to be" (37). The shock to the eighth-grade boy was profound, for despite his traumatic childhood memories of the destruction of his family by white society, Malcolm X had embraced the white success ethic by the time he was in junior high school: "I was trying so hard . . . to be white" (31). What follows, in Chapters 3 through 9, is Malcolm X's account of his life as a ghetto hustler, his first "career," just as his role as a Black Muslim minister was to be his second. If Allah preserved him from the fate of an Alger hero or a Booker T. Washington, from a career as a "successful" shoeshine boy or a self-serving member of the "black bourgeoisie" (38), he was nevertheless destined to enact a kind of inverse parody of the white man's rise to success as he sank deeper and deeper into a life of crime.[7] This is the portion of the *Autobiography* that has been singled out for its vividness by the commentators, with the result that the conversion experience and its aftermath in Chapters 10 through 15 have been somewhat eclipsed. It would be possible, of course, to see in the popularity of this section nothing more than the universal appeal of any evocation of low life and evil ways. In addition, this preference may reflect an instinctive attraction to a more personal mode of autobiography with plenty of concrete self-revelation instead of the more formal testimony of an exemplary life. Certainly Alex Haley responded strongly to this narrative, and so did Malcolm X, though he tried to restrain himself:

> Then it was during recalling the early Harlem days that Malcolm X really got carried away. One night, suddenly, wildly, he jumped up from his chair and, incredibly, the fearsome black demagogue was scat-singing and popping his fingers, "re-bop-de-bop-blap-blam—" and then grabbing a vertical pipe with one hand (as the girl partner) he went jubilantly lindy-hopping around, his coattail and the long legs and the big feet flying as they had in those Harlem days. And then almost as suddenly, Malcolm X caught himself and sat back down, and for the rest of that session he was decidedly grumpy. (391)

Haley captures here the characteristic drama of the autobiographical act that the juxtaposition of the self as it is and as it was inevitably generates. Malcolm X's commitment to his public role as "the fearsome black demagogue" conflicts with his evident pleasure in recapturing an earlier and distinctly personal identity, the historical conked and zooted lindy champ of the Roseland Ballroom in Roxbury, the hustling hipster of Small's Paradise in Harlem.

If the *Autobiography* had ended with the fourteenth or fifteenth chapter, what we would have, I suggest, is a narrative which could be defined as an extremely conventional example of autobiographical form distinguished chiefly by the immediacy and power of its imaginative recreation of the past.[8] It is true that this much of the *Autobiography* would usefully illustrate the survival of the classic pattern of conversion narrative in the contemporary literature of spiritual autobiography, but this interest would necessarily be a limited one given Malcolm X's reticence about the drama of the experience of conversion itself. For Malcolm X the fact of conversion is decisive, life-shaping, identity-altering, but unlike the most celebrated spiritual autobiographers of the past he chooses not to dramatize the experience itself or to explore its psychological dynamics.[9]

III

It seems probable that when Malcolm X began his dictations to Haley in 1963 he anticipated that his narrative would end with an account of his transformation into the national spokesman of Elijah Muhammad's Nation of Islam (the material covered in Chapters 14 and 15 of Haley's text). This was not destined to be the end of the story, however, for the pace of Malcolm X's history, always lively, became tumultuous in 1963 and steadily accelerated until his assassination in 1965. In this last period Malcolm X was to experience two events that destroyed the very premises of the autobiography he had set out to write. The most well-known convert to the Black Muslim religion was first to break with Elijah Muhammad (Chapter 16, "Out") and then to make a pilgrimage to Mecca (Chapter 17), where he underwent a second conversion to what he now regarded as the true religion of Islam. The revelation that Elijah Muhammad was a false prophet shattered the world of Malcolm X and the shape of the life he had been living for twelve years:

> I was like someone who for twelve years had had an inseparable, beautiful marriage—and then suddenly one

morning at breakfast the marriage partner had thrust across the table some divorce papers.

I felt as though something in *nature* had failed, like the sun or the stars. It was that incredible a phenomenon to me—something too stupendous to conceive. (304)

The autobiographical fiction of the completed self was exploded for good, although Malcolm X, with a remarkable fidelity to the truth of his past, was to preserve the fragments in the earlier chapters of the *Autobiography*, as we have seen.

The illumination at Mecca made Malcolm X feel "like a complete human being" for the first time "in my thirty-nine years on this earth" (365), and he assumed a new name to symbolize this new sense of identity, El-Hajj Malik El-Shabazz. In the final chapters of the book (18 and 19) we see Malcolm X in the process of discarding the "old 'hate' and 'violence' image" (423) of the militant preacher of Elijah Muhammad's Nation of Islam, but before he created a design for the life of this new self he was brutally gunned down on February 21, 1965. In fact, it is not at all certain that Malcolm X would have arrived at any single, definitive formulation for the shape of his life even if he had continued to live. In the final pages of the last chapter he observes:

No man is given but so much time to accomplish whatever is his life's work. My life in particular never has stayed fixed in one position for very long. You have seen how throughout my life, I have often known unexpected drastic changes. (378)

With these words Malcolm X articulates a truth already latent but ungrasped in the autobiographical narrative he originally set out to write in his evangelical zeal: his life was not now and never had been a life of the simpler pattern of the traditional conversion story.

Because this complex vision of his existence is clearly not that of the early sections of the *Autobiography*, Alex Haley and Malcolm X were forced to confront the consequences of this discontinuity in perspective for the narrative, already a year old. It was Haley who raised the issue when he learned, belatedly, of the rift between Malcolm X and Elijah Muhammad, for he had become worried that an embittered Malcolm X might want to rewrite the book from his new perspective, and this at a time when Haley regarded their collaboration as virtually complete ("by now I had the bulk of the needed life story material in hand" [406]). Malcolm X's initial response settled the matter temporarily: "I want the book to be the way it was" (412). Haley's concern, however, was justified, for a few months later, following Malcolm X's journey to Mecca, Haley was "appalled" to find that Malcolm X had "red-inked" many of the places in the manuscript "where he had told of his almost father-and-son relationship with Elijah Muhammad." Haley describes this crisis of the autobiographical act as follows:

> Telephoning Malcolm X, I reminded him of his previous decision, and I stressed that if those chapters contained such telegraphing to readers of what would lie ahead, then the book would automatically be robbed of some of its building suspense and drama. Malcolm X said, gruffly, "Whose book is this?" I told him "yours, of course," and that I only made the objection in my position as a writer. He said that he would have to think about it. I was heart-sick at the prospect that he might want to re-edit the entire book into a polemic against Elijah Muhammad. But late that night, Malcolm X telephoned. "I'm sorry. You're right. I was upset about something. Forget what I wanted changed, let what you already had stand." I never again gave him chapters to review unless I was with him. Several times I would covertly watch him frown and wince as he read, but he never again asked for any change in what he had originally said. (414)

Malcolm X's refusal to change the narrative reflects, finally, his acceptance of change as the fundamental law of existence, and yet, curiously, by the very fidelity of this refusal he secures for the remembered past, and for the acts of memory devoted to it, such measure of permanence as the forms of art afford.[10]

The exchange between the two men poses the perplexing issue of perspective in autobiography with an instructive clarity: to which of an autobiographer's selves should he or even can he be true? What are the strategies by which he may maintain a dual or plural allegiance without compromise to his present vision of the truth? In fact, the restraint of the "telegraphing" does leave the climax intact,[11] and yet Malcolm X's decision not to revise the preceding narrative does not produce the kind of obvious discontinuity in authorial perspective that we might expect as a result. Haley's part in this is considerable, for his contribution to the ultimate shape of the *Autobiography* was more extensive and fundamental than his narrowly literary concerns here with foreshadowing and suspense might seem to suggest. Despite his tactful protest that he was only a "writer," Haley himself had been instrumental in the playing out of the autobiographical drama between one Malcolm X, whose faith in Elijah Muhammad had supplied him with his initial rationale for an autobiography, and another, whose repudiation of Elijah Muhammad made the *Autobiography* the extraordinary human document it eventually became. If the outcome of this drama was formalized in Malcolm X's expulsion from the Nation of Islam, it was already in the wind by the time the dictations began in earnest in 1963. Alex Haley was one to read between the lines.

Haley recalls in the "Epilogue" that at the very outset of the project he had been in fundamental disagreement with Malcolm X about the narrative he would help him write. He reports that Malcolm X wanted the focus to be on Elijah Muhammad and the Nation of Islam: "He would bristle when I tried to urge him that the proposed book was *his* life" (388). At this early stage of the collaboration Haley portrays two Malcolms: a loyal public Malcolm X describing a religious movement in which he casts himself in a distinctly subordinate and self-effacing role, and a subversive private Malcolm X scribbling a trenchant counter-commentary in telegraphic red-ink ball point on any available scrap of paper. Determined to feature this second Malcolm X in the autobiography, Haley lured this suppressed identity out into the open by leaving white paper napkins next to Malcolm X's coffee cup to tap his closed communications with himself. Haley carefully retrieved this autobiographical fall-out, and taking his cue from one of these napkin revelations, interestingly about women, Haley "cast a bait" (389) with a question about Malcolm X's mother. Haley reports that with this textbook display of Freudian savvy he was able to land the narrative he was seeking:

From this stream-of-consciousness reminiscing I finally got out of him the foundation for this book's beginning chapters, "Nightmare" and "Mascot." After that night, he never again hesitated to tell me even the most intimate details of his personal life, over the next two years. His talking about his mother triggered something. (390–91)

From the very earliest phase of the dictations, then, the autobiography began to take on a much more personal and private coloration than Malcolm X originally intended. What Elijah Muhammad accomplished, autobiographically speaking, when he "silenced" Malcolm X, was to legitimatize the private utterance of the napkins which had already found its way into the mainstream of a narrative initially conceived as an orthodox work of evangelical piety. After his separation from the Nation of Islam, Malcolm X comments that he began "to think for myself," "after twelve years of never thinking for as much as five minutes about myself" (306). Haley reports two napkin messages of this period that signal the consequences of Malcolm X's new sense of himself and his power for the nearly completed *Autobiography*:

He scribbled one night, "You have not converted a man because you have silenced him. John Viscount Morley." And the same night, almost illegibly, "I was going downhill until he picked me up, but the more I think of it, we picked each other up." (406)[12]

Not only was Malcolm X rejecting the simple clarity of the original conversion narrative he had set out to tell, but he was no longer disposed to sacrifice to the greater glory of Elijah Muhammad his own agency in the working out of his life story.

IV

In the final chapters of the *Autobiography* and in the "Epilogue," as Malcolm X moves toward a new view of his story as a life of changes, he expresses an impressive, highly self-conscious awareness of the problems of autobiographical narrative, and specifically of the complex relationship between living a life and writing an autobiography. All of his experience in the last packed months, weeks, and days of his life worked to destroy his earlier confident belief in the completed self, the completed life, and hence in the complete life story. Thus he writes to Haley in what is possibly his final statement about the *Autobiography*: "I just want to read it one more time because I don't expect to read it in finished form" (426). As Malcolm X saw it at the last, all autobiographies are by nature incomplete and they cannot, accordingly, have a definitive shape. As a life changes, so any sense of the shape of a life must change; the autobiographical process evolves because it is part of the life, and the identity of the autobiographical "I" changes and shifts. Pursuing the logic of such speculations, Malcolm X even wonders whether any autobiography can keep abreast of the unfolding of personal history: "How is it possible to write one's autobiography in a world so fast-changing as this" (408)? And so he observes to Haley, "I hope the book is proceeding rapidly, for events concerning my life happen so swiftly, much of what has already been written can easily be outdated from month to month. In life, nothing is permanent; not even life itself" (413–14).

At the end, then, Malcolm X came to reject the traditional autobiographical fiction that the life comes first, and then the writing of the life; that the life is in some sense complete and that the autobiographical process simply records the final achieved shape. This fiction is based upon a suspension of time,[13] as though the "life," the subject, could sit still long enough for the autobiographical "I," the photographer, to snap its picture. In fact, as Malcolm X was to learn, the "life" itself will not hold still; it changes, shifts position. And as for the autobiographical act, it requires much more than an instant of time to take the picture, to write the story. As the act of composition extends in time, so it enters the life-stream, and the fictive separation between life and life story, which is so convenient—even necessary—to the writing of autobiography, dissolves.

Malcolm X's final knowledge of the incompleteness of the self is what gives the last pages of the *Autobiography* together with the "Epilogue" their remarkable power: the vision of a man whose swiftly unfolding career has outstripped the possibilities of the traditional autobiography he had meant to write. It is not in the least surprising that Malcolm X's sobering insights into the limitations of autobiography are accompanied by an increasingly insistent desire to disengage himself from the ambitions of the autobiographical process. Thus he speaks of the *Autobiography* to Haley time and again as though, having disabused himself of any illusion that the narrative could keep pace with his life, he had consigned the book to its fate, casting it adrift as hopelessly obsolete. Paradoxically, nowhere does the book succeed, persuade, more than in its confession of failure as autobiography. This is the fascination of *The Education of Henry Adams*, and Malcolm X, like Adams, leaves behind him the husks of played-out autobiographical paradigms. The indomitable reality of the self transcends and exhausts the received shapes for a life that are transmitted by the culture, and yet the very process of discarding in itself works to structure an apparently shapeless experience. Despite—or because of—the intractability of life to form, the fiction of the completed self, which lies at the core of the autobiographical enterprise, cannot be readily dispatched. From its ashes, phoenix-like, it reconstitutes itself in a new guise. Malcolm X's work, and Adams' as well, generate a sense that the uncompromising commitment to the truth of one's own nature, which requires the elimination of false identities and careers one by one, will yield at the last the pure ore of a final and irreducible selfhood. This is the ultimate autobiographical dream.

Notes

6. Although Malcolm X's *Autobiography* resembles the traditional conversion narrative in many ways, there are important differences as well. For example, it is somewhat misleading to speak, as Mandel does (272), of Malcolm X's first conversion to the Muslim faith of Elijah Muhammad as the typical "false conversion" of spiritual autobiography. A "false conversion" is usually presented as false by the man who has since found the true faith. This is not Malcolm X's treatment, for in his case the "false conversion" is only partly false, and hence not to be wholly rejected (as the older Jonathan Edwards rejected the miserable seeking of his youth). Again, Mandel pushes these correspondences too far when he identifies the "tension" of the last pages of the *Autobiography* as an expression of the familiar post-conversion fears of "back-sliding" (272–73). Malcolm X knew that Elijah Muhammad had sentenced him to death.

7. In "Malcolm X: Mission and Meaning," *Yale Review*, 56 (1966), Robert Penn Warren reads Malcolm X as a success in the Alger tradition (161–162), and he notes that, setting aside the hatred of the Black Muslims for white society, their values of temperance and hard work resemble the virtues that have made the white middle-class what it is (165). Ohmann stresses Malcolm X's story as a "parodic inversion" (136) of the success story, and she adds that Malcolm X himself later recognized it as such (137).

8. To describe this first part of the *Autobiography* as conventional is by no means to deny the importance of Malcolm X's first conversion as a milestone in the rise of black self-consciousness in America. In the two recent studies of black American autobiography, however, this is not the guiding perspective. Sidonie Smith, in *Where I'm Bound: Patterns of Slavery and Freedom in Black American Autobiography* (Westport, Conn.: Greenwood Press, 1974), reads the experience with the Nation of Islam as the third in a continuing series of disillusionments teaching Malcolm X that "his freedom within the community is finally only a chimera" (96–97). In *Black Autobiography in America* (Amherst: University of Massachusetts Press, 1974), on the other hand, Stephen Butterfield places Malcolm X's Black Muslim phase in the larger context of his development as a black revolutionary: "Malcolm X, pimp and drug pusher, convict, Muslim minister, Pan-Africanist, pilgrim to Mecca, lifting himself up to become one of the few men who could have been the Lenin of America before he was cut down by gunfire" (184).

9. Ohmann interprets the reticence of Malcolm X on the subjective nature of his conversion experience (139–40) as a manifestation of his "distrust of the inner life, even an antipathy to it" (134).

10. In his essay "Modern Black Autobiography in the Tradition," Michael G. Cooke argues that rewriting is an "essential issue for

autobiography" and one unaccountably neglected by students of the form (in *Romanticism: Vistas, Instances, Continuities*, ed. David Thorburn and Geoffrey Hartman [Ithaca, New York: Cornell University Press, 1973], p. 259). Cooke concludes that "the distinctive feature of the *Autobiography* [*of Malcolm X*] is its naturalistic use of time, the willingness to let the past stand as it was, in its own season, even when later developments, of intellect or intuition or event, give it a different quality" (274). Francis R. Hart writes, in "Notes for an Anatomy of Modern Autobiography," that "the autobiographer has always had to consider how to manage, and whether to dramatize, the discontinuities inherent in autobiographical recreation," and he sees Malcolm X as facing this problem courageously and creatively (*New Literary History*, 1 [1970], 489, 501).

11. Malcolm X alludes specifically to the impending crisis in Chapter 12, pp. 197–98, 210; in Chapter 14, pp. 264–65; and in Chapter 15, p. 287. For instances of an undercurrent of retrospective criticism of Elijah Muhammad, see Chapter 10, p. 168 (his false teaching); Chapter 11, pp. 187, 189 (his immorality); Chapter 14, p. 248 (his insecurity); p. 252 (his worth as a leader). These passages, reflecting as they do Malcolm X's altered vision of the man he had formerly worshiped, are presumably interpolations from a later phase of the dictations.

12. The second of the two messages reformulates and repudiates the original dedication of the *Autobiography*.

13. See Cooke, pp. 259–60, on "the problem of the self and time" in autobiography.

H. PORTER ABBOTT ON ORGANIC FORM

In his Epilogue to *The Autobiography of Malcolm X*, Haley writes of the difficulty he had in getting Malcolm on the track of his childhood. Finally, exhausted by the continual polemic of his self-protective and untrusting subject, Haley, in an inspired moment, asked the simple question: "I wonder if you'd tell me something about your mother?" It turned out to be the key, and from that moment on Malcolm delivered in a kind of flood details from his life which, as he says, he had not thought about since they had happened.

The case might be made, I imagine, that Malcolm's mother played as important a role in the story of his conversion as St. Augustine's mother played in that of her son, but the attempt would involve a good deal of sheer speculation and ingenuity, given the material we have. It may also be that there is some underground connection between Malcolm's feeling for his mother and his extreme distrust of women. But, again, to make the case would require the recovery of details and a psychology which far exceed the text we have: in short, another life story. In this life story, the aspects of his mother which are allowed to emerge are allowed to do so precisely because of the powerfully teleological character of the life that is told—as it is conceived by the man who lived it.

> She was always standing over the stove, trying to stretch whatever we had to eat. We stayed so hungry that we were dizzy. I remember the color of dresses she used to wear—they were a kind of faded-out gray. (p. 390)

These are the first details of his life that Haley was permitted to know. They introduce the subject that dominates the first fourteen years of Malcolm's recalled life—the disintegration of his family—in which his mother was so central a figure by her efforts to keep the family together that she became a symbol both of the effort and the disintegration. Because of the converted awareness of the man who left prison in 1952, the long, painful deterioration that his memory organizes around his mother achieves its distinctive emphasis. For the destruction of the black family is now understood as a major instrument in the exertion of control by the white devil, a crime second only to the outright murder of black people (underscored at the outset of Malcolm's account by the killing of his black nationalist father), and a continual repetition in modern America of the original separation of fathers, mothers, sisters and brothers effected by the slave trade. By first destroying his strong, dominating father, white men had removed what little center of gravity the family had had. What was left was gradually eroded by want—itself a product of their earning power as black people—and white social workers who placed the children in separate families and finally had their mother declared mentally unbalanced and committed to an institution.

After Malcolm's Roxbury "conversion" from provincial hick to urban hepcat, the closest he comes to anything like family is—like that conversion, pure parody—an efficiently organized band of thieves which, as far as one can tell from his account, functioned solely for gain. It was "like a family unit," Malcolm recalls, and Malcolm was its cunning and despotic *pater familias*. Later, after leaving prison, he is powerfully moved when he visits his brother Wilfred's Muslim family. His brother's family is impeccably ordered, its movement through the phases of the day controlled by Muslim ritual, its center of authority unambiguously located in the father. Malcolm devotes no little space to the description of this harmonious order, an order which he will later try to maintain in his own family. It is a recovery of the birthright denied him by white culture, just as, in the Black Muslim social program, it is at once a symbolic and practical aspect of the recovery of black dignity.

The Black Muslim prohibition against eating pork is another aspect of the faith that ties back to Malcolm's mother. He recalls repeatedly his mother's fondness for dietary restrictions, particularly her aversion to pork—a cause both of friction with her husband ("a real Georgia Negro" who "believed in eating plenty of what we in Harlem today call 'soul food'") and her conversion to Seventh Day Adventism. It is pretty clear that her objection to pork is, like that of the Black Muslims, based in part on a repudiation of a black stereotype. But it is precisely this repudiation that, as Malcolm recalls, earns for her the label of insanity from the same social workers who eventually managed to dismantle the family:

> I'm not sure just how or when the idea was first dropped by the social workers that our mother was losing her mind.
>
> But I can distinctly remember hearing "crazy" applied to her by them when they learned that the Negro farmer who was in the next house down the road from us had offered to give us some butchered pork—a whole pig, maybe even two of them—and she refused. We all heard

them call my mother "crazy" to her face for refusing good meat. It meant nothing to them even when she explained that we had never eaten pork, that it was against her religion as a Seventh Day Adventist. (p. 17)

When Malcolm is finally taken from his mother and placed in another home, his mother's parting words are, "Don't let them feed him any pig" (p. 19). Eleven years later, when Malcolm's brother Reginald sends him the letter that begins his conversion, its cryptic message is simply, "Malcolm, don't eat any more pork, and don't smoke any more cigarettes. I'll show you how to get out of prison" (p. 155). His mother's command is finally carried out, and by his own account Malcolm was never again to eat pork in his life. Whether or not the original command was a subliminal cause of this repudiation of pork, it is quite clearly his religious awakening and his new concept of black manhood that leads Malcolm to isolate this feature of his mother in the few pages he devotes to her.

There are two other distinctive features of his mother that Malcolm chooses to isolate—her clairvoyance and her mixed blood—and it is worth noting that they also initiate themes in the developing structure of his recollections. Unlike Augustine's mother, whose dreams foretold her son's greatness, Malcolm's mother has waking visions of impending events, a power that Malcolm claims to have inherited and that serves him well during his life as a hustler and a mobster in keeping him alive. It is a motif which prepares critically for his vision in jail of W. D. Fard, the teacher of Elijah Muhammad.

About her mixed blood, Malcolm says that his mother could pass for white:

Her father *was* white. She had straight black hair, and her accent did not sound like a Negro's. Of this white father of hers, I knew nothing except her shame about it. I remember hearing her say she was glad that she had never seen him. It was, of course, because of him that I got my reddish-brown "mariny" color of skin, and my hair of the same color. I was the lightest child in our family. (p. 2)

Ironically, Malcolm's father, the very black black nationalist, is as emotionally unenlightened on this issue as he is on the issue of pork. Malcolm senses that his father favored him for his lighter skin, just as his light-skinned mother whipped him the harder for it. In the hands of the inevitable social workers, the fact becomes a tool for their grim work: ". . . talking to us children, they began to plant the seeds of division in our minds. They would ask such questions as who was smarter than the other. And they would ask me why I was 'so different' " (p. 17).

In the reversal of color value that he experiences through conversion, the American Negro's admixture of white blood shifts from a touch of class to both the sign and actual presence of the devil invading the arteries of a divine race. His attempts at white mimicry—the straightening of his hair, the preference for white women—throughout his descent through Roxbury and Harlem had been an unconscious worship of evil, blindness to the just evaluation his mother had made of his grandfather.

The themes that Malcolm's mother introduces are so richly developed in his autobiography that a discussion of them might quickly become labored. Let me take instead two passages from his early recollections to help make my point. The first comes from Malcolm's junior high school experiences in Mason, Michigan. The general subject is his membership in the basketball team, but the item he features in recalling that subject is the conventional dance held after games in neighboring towns.

Whenever our team walked into another school's gym for the dance, with me among them, I could feel the freeze. It would start to ease as they saw that I didn't try to mix, but stuck close to someone on our team, or kept to myself. I think I developed ways to do it without making it obvious. Even at our own school, I could sense it almost as a physical barrier, that despite all the beaming and smiling, the mascot wasn't supposed to dance with any of the white girls.

It was some kind of psychic message—not just from them, but also from within myself. . . . I would just stand around and smile and talk and drink punch and eat sandwiches, and then I would make some excuse and get away early. (p. 30)

The recollection is followed by a note on what he calls "a peculiar thing. Many of these Mason white boys, like the ones at the Lansing school—especially if they knew me well, and if we hung out a lot together—would get me off in a corner somewhere and push me to proposition certain white girls, sometimes their own sisters" (p. 30).

If one keeps this passage in mind as one moves past the first radical change in Malcolm's style of living and into his life in the Roxbury section of Boston, it helps establish an almost perfectly symmetrical composition in black and white. For the central events of that life are the dances at the Roseland in which, by his own account, Malcolm became something of a star performer. His narration of this period comes to a head with his discovery of Laura, the innocent black girl from Roxbury's middle-class Wambeck and Humboldt Avenue Hill section, whom he introduces to the Roseland. As it turns out, she is a born dancer, and on their second night out she is the feature attraction: "The spotlight was working mostly just us. . . . Her hair was all over her face, it was running sweat, and I couldn't believe her strength. The crowd was shouting and stomping. A new favorite was being discovered; there was a wall of noise around us." But it is just beyond this point, when they leave the dance floor and are being mobbed by the crowd, that Malcolm discovers Sophia:

One bunch of the crowd swarmed Laura; they had her clear up off her feet. And I was being pounded on the back . . . when I caught this fine blonde's eyes. . . . This one I'd never seen among the white girls who came to the Roseland black dances. She was eyeing me levelly. . . .

It's shameful to admit, but I had just about forgotten Laura when she got loose from the mob and rushed up, big-eyed—and stopped. I guess she saw what there was to see in that girl's face—and mine—as we moved out to dance. (pp. 66–67)

Sophia doesn't dance too well, but as Malcolm comments, "Who cared? I could feel the staring eyes of other couples around us." He takes Laura home in a taxi and rushes back to where Sophia is waiting five blocks down from the Roseland. "She had a low convertible. She knew where she was going. Beyond Boston, she pulled off into a side road, and then off that into a deserted lane. And turned off everything but the radio" (p. 67).

Together, the two episodes express more effectively than any analysis the developing structure of this fifteen-year-old mind. They are not only expressive in themselves of the disease which Malcolm, in retrospect, sees that he suffered during his youth, but they lock together in a pattern of contrasts to show its variations. It is a checkerboard pattern which he has already introduced through the feelings of his black father and light mother for his own light skin and which he will develop in a bizarre variation when he calls to memory the bordellos of Harlem where successful white executives pay to be beaten by the blackest prostitutes. In his account of his dancing career, all that remains to embellish that particular pattern of contrast in a kind of coda is for Malcolm to recall how, later still, he paid his respects to Mason in "My sharkskin gray 'Cab Calloway' zoot suit, the long, narrow, knob-toed shoes, and the four-inch brimmed pearl-gray hat over my conked fire-red hair":

> The night before I left, a dance was given in the Lincoln School gymnasium. . . . I'd left Lansing unable to dance, but now I went around the gymnasium floor flinging little girls over my shoulders and hips, showing my most startling steps. Several times the band nearly stopped, and nearly everybody left the floor, watching with their eyes like saucers. (p. 79)

The final passage I want to look at is particularly appropriate to the argument I am proposing because it treats an incident which, at first reading, appears to be an isolated example of the purely anecdotal. I have in mind Malcolm's boxing career, which ran its inglorious course during a few short months of his fourteenth year. It has all the ingredients of a childhood melodrama. Malcolm, defeated badly in his first match by a white boy, trains long and hard for the rematch. He is determined to win. His pride and reputation are at stake. But all there is to Malcolm's second and last fight is the white boy's first punch.

Malcolm gives due thanks to Allah ("I might have wound up punchy"), yet for a moment he had stepped into, and then out of, a classic life story of black achievement. By including this vignette, Malcolm draws attention to the less than orthodox character of his autobiography as a Negro life—the story of a black man who is not only excluded from athletic achievement but who thrives on the superiority of his intelligence. He lives by his wits, cutting against the grain of racial cliché. The motif recurs continually, as for example when Malcolm is matched with a white contestant while working as a sandwich man on the "Yankee Clipper":

> I was working down the aisle and a big, beefy, red-faced cracker soldier got up in front of me, so drunk he was weaving, and announced loud enough that everybody in the car heard him, "I'm going to fight you, nigger." I remember the tension. I laughed and told him, "Sure, I'll fight, but you've got too many clothes on." He had on a big Army overcoat. He took that off, and I kept laughing and said he still had on too many. I was able to keep that cracker stripping off clothes until he stood there drunk with nothing on from his pants up, and the whole car was laughing at him, and some other soldiers got him out of the way. I went on. I never would forget that—that I couldn't have whipped that white man as badly with a club as I had with my mind. (p. 77)

In the art of manipulating appearances, of which Malcolm became a master during his life in the underworlds of Roxbury and Harlem, the white conception of Negro stupidity becomes simply another weapon in his arsenal. With his car full of loot and the police on his tail, Malcolm will flag down the policeman, shuffle over and, "bumbling my words like a confused Negro," ask for directions.

When at last, through his conversion, Malcolm learns of the divine creativity of the black race, the significance of this aspect of his life is made clear. And it is this new vision which makes Cassius Clay's defeat of Sonny Liston so important. Clay was not only a distinct evolutionary advance over the Brown Bomber and Floyd Patterson—who could prove that "mind could win over brawn"—but he was also a Muslim. In recalling his famous visit to the Clay camp in Miami on the eve of the fight, Malcolm works both themes fully:

> I brought from New York with me some photographs of Floyd Patterson and Sonny Liston in their fight camps, with white priests as their "spiritual advisors." Cassius Clay, being a Muslim, didn't need to be told how white Christianity had dealt with the American black man. "This fight is the *truth*," I told Cassius. "It's the Cross and the Crescent fighting in a prize ring—for the first time. It's a modern Crusades—a Christian and a Muslim facing each other with television to beam it off Telstar for the whole world to see what happens!" I told Cassius, "Do you think Allah has brought about all this intending for you to leave the ring as anything but the champion?" (You may remember that at the weighing-in, Cassius was yelling such things as "It is prophesied for me to be successful! I cannot be beaten!") (pp. 306–307).

There are, of course, limits to the emphasis Malcolm can place on the foreordination of this event, because in order to bring off the synthesis he requires, it must be patently clear that "the secret of one of fight history's greatest upsets was that months before that night, Clay had out-thought Liston" (p. 308).

In its broadest terms, my argument so far is that spontaneous production of organic literary form need not be a romantic cliché but a serious hypothesis in the study of autobiography. Though Malcolm really underwent not one but two religious conversions during his life, I have concentrated on the effects of the first—his conversion to the Muslim faith of Elijah Muhammad—because it is the informing event which dominates most of the narrative with which he provides Haley. I have focussed on it to show that the organic wholeness of an autobiography can, at least in the case of a convert, spring directly from the strength of focus endowed him by his conversion—that, in the case of Malcolm X, it is what allowed him to winnow, without forethought, almost 14,000 days of his life. This is not to say, of course, that an autobiographer might not imitate organic structure in the details of his life with the most consummate awareness of his formal enterprise. It is simply to argue that such structure need not be a learned aspect of autobiography or the result of literary self-consciousness, but a direct product of the God-given character of the mind as it reflects upon itself. . . .

. . . Just as Black Muslim exegetes use the Bible and the work of such Christians as Rutherford and Frank Norris to reveal a message often directly opposed to that of the Christian interpreter, so, too, did the gnostics. The new reading is sanctioned by a divine gift of allegorical interpretation. And as Hans Jonas has argued, the method is an index of the revolutionary character of the religion:

> Instead of taking over the value-system of the traditional myth, it proves the deeper "knowledge" by reversing the roles of good and evil, sublime and base, blest and accursed, found in the original. It tries, not to demonstrate agreement, but to shock by blatantly subverting the meaning of the most firmly established, and preferably also the most revered, elements of tradition. The rebellious tone of this type of allegory cannot be missed, and it therefore is one of the expressions of the revolutionary position which Gnosticism occupies in late classical culture.[11]

Thus, for example, the wicked lord of this world accepts the horrible sacrifice of Abel. And thus, according to Elijah Muhammad, the power of blackness is the true power of

God. Malcolm, when he is first thrown into prison, fulfills the traditional paradox of the "way down" by so cursing the Bible and God that he earns the name of "Satan." In retrospect, it is seen as a form of ripening. By becoming the "worst kind of nigger," he shortens the distance to that final reversal in which his divinity is revealed to him along with knowledge of who the real Satan is.

But it is in its dualistic, and primarily substantialistic, conceptions of good and evil that, for our purposes at least, the religion of W. D. Fard most significantly mirrors the religion of Mani. The colors are reversed, but the thinking is the same. For Malcolm it provided a framework within which he could exercise his organizational and rhetorical genius. There is little doubt that Malcolm X was the driving force behind the massive growth of the Black Muslim faith between 1952 and 1963, and the power of his appeal lay in his ability to exploit an elementary division of the world—which for the great mass of black people was a simple fact of their existence—and to confer on it a new valuation. But the important point is that the efficiency with which Malcolm moved others derived from an efficiency that operated in his own mind, an efficiency which, like that of the Manichaeans which appealed so to the young Augustine, appealed both because of its simplicity and because of its power of keeping his character intact.

Malcolm could speak of a "pre-Islamic submission" as if there were a self within his self, acting of its own will, but generally when he looks back over his life the effect of his dualistic and strongly providential faith is to cast it as a series of actions and reactions carried out in blindness. He follows in his memory the inmate's exploration of the prison-house, noting continually how little the inmate understood the character of his prison. The organicism achieved is thus inevitably thematic. Where Augustine, the monist and believer in free choice, features the causal stages in which his soul collaborates with the Lord, Malcolm features the thematic unity of his life before the sudden swift change which came with the gnosis. His conversion in this way orders what had been chaos. It allows him to make sense of his privation and clarifies a history of suffering which, in his ignorance, he had not even understood as suffering.

Note
11. Hans Jonas, *The Gnostic Religion* (Boston: Beacon Press, 1963), p. 92.

JOHN EDGAR WIDEMAN ON VOICE AND AUTHORIAL PRESENCE IN THE BOOK

What's striking about Alex Haley's *Autobiography of Malcolm X* is [that] Haley presents a "talking head," first-person narration recorded from the fixed perspective of a single video camera. With a few small and one very large exception to this rule— the Epilogue . . . —what we get from first to last page of the *Autobiography* is one voice addressing us, an extended monologue, sermon rap, recollection in tranquility of the awesome variety and precipitous turnabouts of Malcolm's life. The enormous popular success of the autobiography (millions of copies sold and selling), the power and persistence of the image of Malcolm it achieves, makes it worthwhile to investigate how Haley does so much with so little fuss, how an approach that appears rudimentary in fact conceals sophisticated choices, quiet mastery of a medium.

First, what does the exception tell us about the rules? Though the Epilogue was written after Malcolm's death and focuses upon his assassination and its aftermath, it remains a record of life as much as death, a concrete manifestation of how a spirit transcends the physical body's passing if the spirit's force continues to touch those who loved it, or those who didn't love but can't forget its impact, its continuing presence. Appended to the *Autobiography*, the Epilogue in many reader's minds blends with Malcolm's story, becomes part of the "as told to," a further conversation between the writer and Malcolm, Malcolm and the reader in spite of the attempt of Malcolm's enemies to silence him.

Several new, important subjects are introduced in the Epilogue: the writer of the *Autobiography*, the process of constructing the book, the relationship between writer and subject. Haley utilizes a variety of narrative modes and devices in the Epilogue. He inserts himself into the story, describes how, where, and why Malcolm is speaking, Malcolm's appearance, state of mind. Haley quotes, summarizes, cites other sources for points of view on Malcolm, ventures his own analysis and opinions explicitly in first person. This mixed form of narrative exposition is handled quite adroitly. The Epilogue becomes an eloquent extension of the *Autobiography*, a gripping, dramatically structured fugue that impels the reader toward the climax of assassination, the inevitable slow shock of recognition afterward as the world assesses the loss of Malcolm. Nearly one-sixth of the *Autobiography* (74 pages out of 456—a 4-page comment by Ossie Davis, a 6-page Introduction by M. S. Handler complete the volume), the Epilogue is proof positive that Haley's choice of a "talking head" for the body of his book was not chosen because he couldn't compose in another fashion.

"Nothing can be in this book's manuscript that I didn't say, and nothing can be left out that I want in" (*Autobiography*, 387). Malcolm insisted this guarantee be part of the contract between Haley and himself. In return Haley received a pledge from Malcolm to "give me a priority quota of his time for the planned 100,000 word 'as told to' book," and later Haley asked for and tells us he received from Malcolm permission to write "comments of my own about him which would not be subject to his review." How Malcolm's death affected this bargain, what kind of book his final cut of the manuscript might have produced, we can only guess. We could have posed this question to Haley, but now he's gone too. However, the nature of writing biography or autobiography or any kind of writing means that Haley's promise to Malcolm, his intent to be a "dispassionate chronicler," is a matter of disguising, not removing, his authorial presence.

Allowing Malcolm to speak for himself meant constructing a text that *seems* to have no author (in a first draft I slipped and wrote "*no other*"), that *seems* to speak for itself without mediation. I've encountered many readers who experienced the book in just such a fashion, who were surprised when reminded of Alex Haley's role. Calling the book an autobiography is of course an explicit denial of an authorial presence and encourages this reaction in readers. Yet as we should have learned from Afro-American folklore or from novelists such as James Joyce who confess the secrets of their craft, effacing the self is also a way of empowering, enabling the self. If you're skillful enough at the sleight-of-hand of storytelling (witness Charles Chesnut's "Uncle Julius"), you can disappear, charm your audience into forgetting you're there, behind and within the tale, manipulating your audience, silently paring your fingernails. Haley performs a double-dip, disappears twice. Once into Malcolm and again with Malcolm as Malcolm the monologist, oracular teacher/preacher, the bardic bluesman who knows there because he goes there, Malcolm the storyteller collapses distance between teller and tale, tale and audience.

In the *Autobiography* Malcolm's voice issues from no particular place, no particular body, no particular time. The locus of the voice is his mind, and of course the mind can routinely accomplish what the most sophisticated experiments in written narrative can only suggest and mimic: flashback, flashforward, a seamless flow/exchange between inner and outer worlds, great leaps from location to location, lightning switches between levels of diction and discourse, switches in verb tense, grammatical person, time-space elisions, characters bursting into a scene full blown, announcing, establishing their intricate histories, their physical appearance with a single word. So it's not exactly as if Haley has narrowed his options by situating and representing the *Autobiography* as the first-person flow of Malcolm's speech and thought. Haley grants Malcolm the tyrannical authority of an author, a disembodied speaker whose implied presence blends into the reader's imagining of the tale being told.

Physical descriptions the *Autobiography*'s speaker offers of himself are "time capsules" scattered through the narrative, snapshots of how he appeared at various periods in his life, the boy with "reddish brown mariny color" of skin and hair, the conked teenager in zoot suit and knobby-toed shoes. The voice presently speaking is as generic as the business suits Malcolm X wore as a minister delivering the Honorable Elijah Muhammad's message. Yet the voice also gains a larger-than-life status as it gradually usurps our attention. We make up a body to match the deeds being described, a body substantiated by our participation, identification. No actor could ever match the image of the Lone Ranger I conjured as a kid listening to the masked man's adventures on the radio (who knows, part of the attraction, part of me may have been seeing part of him as black) so I never cared much for the disappointing version of the masked rider that eventually appeared in a TV series.

Haley's disappearance into Malcolm's voice permits readers to accomplish an analogous disappearing act. We open the boundaries of our identities, we're suspended, taken up to the higher ground of Malcolm's voice as a congregation is drawn into the crystal-clear parables and anecdotes of a righteous sermon. We recognize ourselves in what's being said. We amen it. Speaking for us as well as to us, the voice attains the godlike veracity and authority conventionally attributed to the third-person omniscient mode of history texts. The story becomes our story; we manufacture a presence to fill the space Haley seems to have left undefined, unoccupied. Of course some readers, fewer and fewer now, would bring living memories of Malcolm to their reading, and many would have seen photos or films, but these fragments don't alter the rhetorical design of the book and may even enhance it because the *Autobiography*'s omnipresence, its compelling version of its subject, continues to influence images of Malcolm preserved in other media.

Haley's choice of standard English for Malcolm's voice sustains the identification, the exchange between speaker and audience. Vernacular expressions, idiomatic, traditional formulas of African-American speech, occur infrequently in the *Autobiography*, and usually appear within quotes, italics, marked explicitly to indicate that the speaker is abandoning his chosen register. Conservative as the device of a talking head, the strategy of mainstreaming Malcolm's voice is just as quietly effective. The blandness of the language of the *Autobiography* invites the reader not to perform it, but ignore it. The choice of a particular black vernacular would have raised questions of class, as well as race, potentially divisive issues. Would Malcolm be speaking only *for* and *to* those people who speak like him? Would a publisher try to sell to predominantly white readers a book in which one black man addresses other black people in terms only partially comprehensible to the white audience? (How gender is implicated raises further issues that won't be addressed here.) Haley finesses potential problems by sticking to transparent, colorless dialect. Words in the *Autobiography* are cloaked in the same sort of invisibility as its author. Haley signals us to read the text as the events of a life, directly told to us by the person who lived it. Someone is talking to us. When we listen, the writing, like the narrator, disappears into the seemingly unmediated report. Haley's genius is to convince us to hear, not read.

Another advantage Haley gains by his choice of the standard English of TV announcers, textbooks, cereal boxes, and most best-sellers is the conspicuous absence of all but the most commonplace, inert, rudimentary figurative language. Attention is drawn to action, to what's being represented, not how it's represented (unless you stubbornly, peevishly insist on asking the latter, often very relevant question). The "personality" of the narrative voice is minimalized, its role as camera eye, objective chronicler, window on reality is enhanced. (Consider the reverse of this process, TV stations juicing up the inert "facts" of weather by foregrounding the "personality" of the weatherperson.) The narrator becomes an unintrusive "voice-over" in the movie the audience constructs from his relation of incidents. If not exactly infallible, the voice Haley fashions for Malcolm has the authority of a courtroom witness, well dressed, articulate, educated, intelligent, one whose account of his experience is seductive, can't be easily discredited or ignored. Another way of saying this is that particular registers of language contain very distinct shorthands or versions of reality, and what's being activated, confirmed when a speaker skillfully manipulates a given register is the world, the assumptions that consenting adults have agreed in advance constitute what's real. Tit for tat the speaker becomes real as he or she verifies the unspoken compact.

Finally, Haley's choice of a voice for Malcolm (himself), because it's designed to transparently reveal what actually happened, can neatly accommodate an audience whose first language may not be standard English. Most African-American readers, whatever registers of English they commonly speak, can amen the familiar people, places, and events of Malcolm's story, can identify with the content of Malcolm's experience, with someone who's been down and out, 'buked and scorned. Many would understand his immersion in the fast life, prison, his religious awakening, his outrage, his simmering frustration and anger toward the American way. The structure of Malcolm's discourse complements its content. The ideological core of the *Autobiography*, the interpretation and analysis of Malcolm's life, would be familiar and convincing to African Americans whose primary mode of communication is oral, not written because in the culture of sermons, blues, street-corner raps, the speaker offers his or her life (our life) as parable, illustration, example, reasoning concretely, directly from the personal to the archetypal, from common nuggets of experience to general principles. Speakers share experiences you share with them. His or her conclusions are seldom surprises. You're taken where you've been. But because nothing is ever exactly repeated, return is not simply repetition, but sometimes often revelation.

That's me he's talking about, singing about, praying about, insulting. Yes. Yes. I was there. It happens just that way, every day. Tell the truth.

CLENORA HUDSON-WEEMS ON MALCOLM'S EVOLVING ATTITUDES ABOUT WOMEN

Street Life

Malcolm's views on women mirrored the particular circumstances of his life. The turning points in his life reflected the turning points in his thinking. During his early years, before his lengthy incarceration for burglary charges, Malcolm Little's attitude toward women in general was negative. Unfortunately, his opinion of women reflects the social influences which shape the attitudes of many Africana men living in a capitalist society. From very early in his adult life, he was the pimp, the hustler, the parasite and the thief, who callously used women for personal gains. Malcolm regarded women as objects reflecting his sexual prowess, most of whom were not to be trusted. He perceived women as capable of depriving men of their masculinity. Hence, out of fear, he would not allow himself to become too emotionally involved with women. In the *Autobiography of Malcolm X*, he asserts,

> I wouldn't have considered it possible for me to love any woman. I'd had too much experience that women were only tricky, deceitful, untrustworthy flesh. I had seen too many men ruined, or at least tied down, or in some other way messed up by women.[8]

For him, they were his partners in sex, dance and crime, but never his equal. He concludes here that,

> The value given to women was as a commodity either to be exploited or displayed as an ornament: A woman was nothing short of a commodity.[9]

During this stage of his development, it was streetlife that sculptured Malcolm's opinion of the woman; for most of his time was spent in the streets and outside of a traditional family structure. In the following passage, he highlights the influence of street life in his socialization:

> It was in this house that I learned more about women than I ever did in any other single place. It was these working prostitutes who schooled me to things that every wife and every husband should know. Later on, it was chiefly the women who weren't prostitutes who

taught me to be very distrustful of most women; there seemed to be a higher code of ethics and sisterliness among those prostitutes than among numerous ladies of the church who have more men for kicks than the prostitutes have for pay.[10]

The interpretation of the streets regarding the question of the White woman in particular dictated that she was a common commodity, one who could also be a status symbol for men. Such was the case with Sophia, the White woman who became the supreme status symbol for Malcolm because of her color. Unfortunately, this position is not unique to Malcolm, for many Africana men share this misguided notion:

Now at that time, in Roxbury, in any black ghetto in America, to have a white woman who wasn't a known common whore was—for the average black man, at least—a status symbol of the first order.[11]

Sophia was the woman for whom Malcolm cruelly dropped his Black girlfriend and dance partner, Laura. Although Malcolm viewed Sophia as a "status symbol," she was to him still just a woman; he saw all women as the same during this time. As for Sophia, however, it turned out that she became his downfall. In spite of the fact that she afforded him material gains in addition to being a status symbol, his use of Sophia and her sister as accomplices in a burglary made his crime even more socially detestable by the White-dominated criminal justice system because of their color. Malcolm received a ten-year sentence for his first-time burglary offense rather than the two years generally established for first-time burglary offenders. However, this incarceration was positive for Malcolm. It set the stage for his social and political evolution. During his incarceration, he was officially introduced to the Nation of Islam, a religion spearheaded by the Honorable Elijah Muhammad. The Nation of Islam mandated that male devotees adopt a different attitude toward women.

Nation of Islam: Religious Fundamentalism

Without question, Malcolm's imprisonment turned out to be a blessing in disguise. It was during this time that his first metamorphosis, both intellectually and spiritually, began to take shape. Paving the way for his intellectual growth was Malcolm's half-sister, Ella. He moved to Boston to live with her after his mother was placed in a mental institution following her husband's lynching and her family's subsequent financial impoverishment. Ella worked diligently towards having Malcolm transferred to the Norfolk Prison, a facility which had an exceptionally good library. Needless to say, Malcolm had tremendous respect for Ella. Long before his incarceration, he describes her as follows:

> . . . [S]he was the first really proud black woman I had ever seen in my life. She was plainly proud of her very dark skin. This was unheard of among Negroes in those days, especially Lansing.[12]

She had a keen influence upon Malcolm's ideas. Her sense of pride indelibly impacted upon his consciousness and her role in facilitating his academic desires was invaluable. Later, when Malcolm severed his ties with the Nation of Islam and organized the Organization of Afro-American Unity (OAAU), he appointed Ella to a high place within the organization. This act demonstrated his regard for his sister in particular and for Africana women.

Without question during Malcolm's imprisonment, his views on the woman took an about face; for example, his attitude toward women shifted from total disrespect and disregard to respect and protection. While he made a shift in attitude, he still held women in a position of subordination to men, which restricted them to the home. This somewhat "improved" attitude toward the woman, uplifting her from abject depravity, was attributed mostly to the Islamic faith, which called for respect for and protection of the woman, although the religion taught and practiced (and still does in some respect) female subjugation. . . .

. . . No longer a hoodlum, the new Malcolm X assumed a more positive posture, one which demanded a new position toward the woman in particular. Nevertheless, his position toward women, as was true of men in general in the Nation of Islam, was still chauvinistic and thus oppressive, believing them to be under the man. His attitude, to be sure, toward the woman was filtered through the practice of Islam, both through the Honorable Elijah Muhammad's version and through orthodox Islam. This view was taught weekly in the Nation of Islam's classes during Malcolm's association with the movement.

> Thursday nights there are the M.G.T. (Muslim Girls' Training) and the G.C.C. (General Civilization Class), where the women and girls of Islam are taught how to keep homes, how to rear children, how to care for husbands, how to cook, sew, how to act at home and abroad, and other things that are important to being a good Muslim sister and mother and wife. . . .
> Fridays are devoted to Civilization Night, when classes are held for brothers and sisters in the area of the domestic relations, emphasizing how both husbands and wives must understand and respect each other's true natures.[13]

As indicated, the chief role of the woman falls under domesticity, such as house cleaning, child rearing, cooking and sewing. Moreover, emphasis is placed on female submissivity, as the woman must be taught to care for and respect her male counterpart as her superior.

In spite of the limitations inflicted upon women, Malcolm, during this stage of his development, demonstrated more respect toward them. Respecting the woman was one of the critical codes of honor for the members of the Nation of Islam:

> Now Islam has very strict laws and teachings about women, the core of them being that the true nature of a man is to be strong, and a woman's true nature is to

be weak, and while a man must at all times respect his woman, at the same time he needs to understand that he must control her if he expects to get her respect.[14]

Whether he truly believed in the limitations of women or not, as dictated by the Nation of Islam, he publicly acted out the philosophy of his religion. Like many Muslim men, Malcolm subjugated the woman by religious tradition. In the writer's opinion, his acts were perhaps not in total accord with his gut thinking. After some time with the Nation of Islam, the more enlightened Malcolm began to redefine and reconcile his views toward women.

Post Nation of Islam: Revolutionary

His first act upon leaving the Nation of Islam was to expose the Honorable Elijah Muhammad's sexual exploitation of some women in the nation of Islam. This response occurred after Malcolm had tried to ignore the rumors surrounding Elijah Muhammad's indiscretion for years. Even when they finally came out in the open, his initial step was to justify them on religious grounds. Muhammad had sired several children by several of his young secretaries, immoral acts to which Malcolm boldly stood in opposition. Malcolm had come to believe that women were deserving of equal respect, a belief which probably had its roots in his early childhood response to the women in his immediate family.

As a contemporary of Nkrumah, Malcolm strongly believed in Nkrumah's words:

The women of Africa have already shown themselves to be of paramount importance in the revolutionary struggle. They gave active support to the independence movement in their various countries, and in some cases their courageous participation in demonstrations and other forms of political action had a decisive effect on the outcome. They have, therefore, a good revolutionary record, and are a great source of power for our politico-military organization. Maximum use must be made of their special skill and potentialities. . . . The degree of a country's revolutionary awareness may be measured by the political maturity of its women.[15]

While these quotations refer specifically to the role of the African woman in the African Revolution, they are also applicable to today's Africana women of the diaspora. Their presence and role are equal to Africana men. Later in his life, Malcolm came to both realize and appreciate the significance of this role.

After several trips to Africa, the motherland of all Africana people, and more significant to Malcolm's change, his trips to Mecca, El-Hajj Malik El-Shabazz emerged as a new personality. His trips to Mecca were a part of fulfilling the pilgrimage requirement demanded of all Moslems. There he received his Hajj and was subsequently required to acquire a religious name. Even today, the status of women of Islamic countries has not changed in any significant way. Their religious role is still limited. However, Malcolm's metamorphosis into one who promoted the woman to the status of equal partner to her male counterpart in the struggle for total liberation became apparent. His visits to his African motherland, especially Ghana, helped to crystallize his view of the Africana woman's role. In his new posture, he demonstrated the writer's present prescription for the existing controversial tension between the Africana man and woman:

a renegotiation of Africana male–female roles in society. In so doing, there must be a call to halt once and for all female subjugation, while continuing the crucial struggle for the liberation of Africana people the world over.[16]

Malcolm came to appreciate the woman as an essential entity in the united efforts in mobilizing and revolutionizing society. In *Malcolm X: The Last Speeches*, Bruce Perry asserts that Malcolm believed that the woman must be respected. Observing the role of women in the National Independence Movements, such as the Tanzania African National Union (TANU) with its women's wing, and the progressive role of women like Shirley Graham Du

Bois, director of Ghanaian television, must have had an impact upon Malcolm's evolving thinking. In fact, Malcolm stated:

[I]t might interest you to know that one of the most progressive moves Ghana has made is to start establishing, installing, a television network. And I was taken through this television studio and plant by Mrs. Du Bois, Dr. W. E. B. Du Bois's wife, who is the director of television in Ghana. She—to my knowledge, she's the only Black director of television in Africa. I may be wrong, but the only one I know of is she. And she's a woman, and she's an Afro-American, and I think that should make Afro-American women mighty proud.[17]

He acknowledged Mrs. Du Bois as a very significant entity in the progress of Africa. Moreover, he made the following observations about her: "She's one of the most intelligent women I've ever met . . ."[18] This statement represents his interest in verbalizing his evolved attitude toward women. In addition to his acknowledgement of Mrs. Du Bois's accomplishments, Malcolm saluted another Black woman, Mrs. Fannie Lou Hamer, a civil rights activist who was a Mississippi Freedom Democratic Party Congressional candidate. He described her as "the country's number one freedom fighting woman."[19] This powerful reference to Mrs. Hamer and her role in the struggle for Black people demonstrates his respect for Africana women. Malcolm evolved to the realization that the woman must be free if Africana people are to truly experience freedom for their family, their community, and their culture. According to Earl Grant, Malcolm's position concerning women and their role in the Organization of Afro-American Unity reflects an organizational indicator of his growth and development on the question of the woman. Malcolm ". . . wanted women to be given a more clearly defined role in the OAAU,"[20] as demonstrated by his later appointment of his sister, Ella, to a key position within the organization.

Moving beyond the American context of women's role, African women were full players in the collective liberation struggle of the men and women on the continent as observed by Malcolm. He saw that the Africana woman was just as much committed to the struggle as the man. In fact, he stated that there were instances when she did more in the struggle than the man. She actively supported independence movements. Moreover, she fearlessly engaged in liberation demonstrations. In view of all this, Malcolm came to understand that it was important that the woman understand the issues confronting her people and threatening their humanity. Hence, Malcolm came to believe that the Africana woman should be educated to combat all forms of ignorance and oppression. At this stage in his consciousness Malcolm's respect for educated and socially conscious women reached its pinnacle.

In an article published about six years after Malcolm's assassination, Betty Shabazz, his widow, reflected on his philosophy position regarding women. She stated that her husband believed the following:

> The black woman has the chief responsibility for passing along black cultural traditions to the children. Malcolm had a tremendous respect for motherhood. . . . The black woman, he believed, is the sustainer of life which she had to be because of circumstance, the emotional supporter of the family, the maintainer and teacher of culture, the vital force in any movement. "If you educate a man," he used to say, "you educate an individual; if you educate a woman, you educate a family."[21]

Malcolm's last statement came from Nkrumah's elder and rival, Dr. Aggrey, a noted African educator, who emphasized the significance of educated African women to the revolutionary struggle. Malcolm respected the woman as the culture-bearer. Shabazz concluded that Malcolm no longer believed that the woman should be limited to the duties of the home. Moreover, she asserted that "in the movement, he felt that a woman's role should be determined by her qualifications. He did not believe that a woman's role was just in the home."[22]

Notes

8. Malcolm X, *The Autobiography of Malcolm X*, Alex Haley, editor (New York: Grove Press, Inc., 1965), p. 226. All subsequent quotation will come from this edition.

9. Malcolm X, p. 134.

10. Malcolm X, p. 91.

11. Malcolm X, pp. 66–67.

12. Malcolm X, p. 32.

13. Malcolm X, p. 227.

14. Malcolm X, p. 226.

15. Kwame Nkrumah, *Handbook of Revolutionary Warfare* (New York: International Publishers, 1968), pp. 89–91.

16. Hudson-Weems, p. 188.

17. Perry, p. 96.

18. Perry, p. 96.

19. George Breitman, editor, *Malcolm X Speaks* (New York: Grove Weidenfeld, 1965), p. 135.

20. George Breitman, editor, *The Last Year of Malcolm X* (New York: Pathfinder, 1969), p. 90.

21. Betty Shabazz, "The Legacy of My Husband Malcolm X," *The Search*, edited by Alma Murray and Robert Thomas (New York: Scholastic Book Services, 1971), pp. 69–72.

22. Betty Shabazz, p. 72.

Works Cited

Breitman, George (Ed.). 1969. *The Last Year of Malcolm X*. New York: Pathfinder.

———. 1965. *Malcolm X Speaks*. New York: Grove Weidenfeld.

Malcolm X. 1965. *The Autobiography of Malcolm X*, Alex Haley (Ed.). New York: Grove Press, Inc.

Hudson-Weems, Clenora. 1989. "Cultural and Agenda Conflicts in Academe: Critical Issues for Africana Women's Studies," *Western Journal of Black Studies*, 13 (Winter): 185–189.

Murray, Alma and Robert Thomas (Eds.). 1971. "The Legacy of My Husband Malcolm X," in *The Search*. New York: Scholastic Book Services, 1971.

Nkrumah, Kwame. 1968. *Handbook of Revolutionary Warfare*. New York: International Publishers.

Morrison, Toni. 1987. *Beloved*. New York: Alfred A. Knopf.

Perry, Bruce (Ed.). 1989. *Malcolm X: The Last Speeches*. New York: Pathfinder.

Sertima, Ivan Van. 1988. *Great Black Legends: Ancient & Modern*. New York: Journal of African Civilizations Ltd., Inc.

CAROL TULLOCH ON FASHION AND DRESS AS A
METAPHOR OF TRANSFORMATION

Spike Lee's 1992 film portrayal of the life of Malcolm X is also based on *The Autobiography of Malcolm X*, and is one of the key players in the celebration of the life of Malcolm X. . . .

The film opens with a carnivalesque night-time vibe of a boisterous, noisy Boston street with all the glamour of Black city life in the early 1940s. The teenager Malcolm Little, or 'Red' as he was rechristened by fellow street revellers, strides across the screen with his 'Homie' Shorty in an outlandish, meticulously styled light blue Zoot suit ensemble:

> the young salesman picked off a rack a Zoot suit that was just wild: sky-blue pants thirty inches in the knee and angle-narrowed down to twelve inches at the bottom, and a long coat that pinched my waist and flared out below my knees. As a gift, the salesman said, the store would give me a narrow leather belt with my initial 'L' on it. Then he said I ought to also buy a hat, and I did—blue, with a feather in the four-inch brim. Then the store gave me another present: a long, thick-lined, gold-plated chain that swung down lower than my coat hem.
>
> (Malcolm X 1968: 135)

Malcolm X devotes a whole page of his autobiography to being 'schooled' in the etiquette of Zoot suit assemblage. The next page details the initiation process of the do-it-yourself 'conk' to complete the transformation of Malcolm Little into Red. In recollection, it was his 'conked' hair, not the image of himself in the Zoot suit, that 'was my first really big step toward self-degradation . . . I admire any Negro man who has never had himself conked, or who has had the sense to get rid of it—as I finally did' (Malcolm X 1968: 138). To go beyond 'the natural' hairstyle and to chemically transform one's birthright and identity as 'black', caused Malcolm X pain that extracted from him a lengthy sermon on racial pride. To wear the Zoot

103

suit, on the other hand, and the elaborate accompanying accoutrements of hat and chains, and lindy-hopping at the Roseland Ballroom, was part of being 'Black'. Malcolm X saw the wearing of the Zoot suit by Black men as staying 'real', 'being their natural selves', not diluting their identity with 'phoney airs' like the 'negroes breaking their backs trying to imitate white people' (Malcolm X 1968: 122–5).

I believe that to straighten one's hair, at this historical moment, and to wear an outlandishly cut and coloured suit were both techniques of self-imaging that did not inhabit different degrees of 'Blackness', but when combined they produced a new, alternative aesthetic of 'Black' cultural experience. None the less, Malcolm X's adherence to a demarcation of ethnic divide based on an authentic Black body aesthetic remained in his analysis of this period of his life. In the opening sequence of *Malcolm X* Lee tried to capture the quintessence of styling and dressing-up amongst young Black men in the early 1940s. It was part of the street culture and camaraderie of these youths who revelled being in the spotlight, and saw themselves as the 'connoisseurs of styles'. As Malcolm X instructed: 'In the ghetto, as in suburbia, it's the same status struggle to stand out in some envied way from the rest' (Malcolm X 1968: 153). When you are 16, as Malcolm X was, the dressed body, the white girlfriend and the dancing were the technologies used in this battle of street status amongst one's peers.

None the less, this exuberant and popularist opening into the very serious issue of who Malcolm X was and is, focuses on his immersion into urban dress and style, and being at the centre of one of the most radically subversive ensembles. An underlying agenda of the Zoot suit was to critique the Second World War, and to question America's moral stance in its defence of other races from inhumane crimes, when it was guilty itself of such occurrences in its own country, such as lynching and the Jim Crow system, against non-whites. To wear such an expanse of fabric as the knee-length, wide-shouldered jacket and voluminous trousers, was to flout the rationing regulations. In the eyes of 'right thinking Americans', this caused one to question the patriotism of its wearer (White and White

1998: 249). From March 1942 the Zoot suit was effectively an illegal ensemble, following a dictate from the War Production Board that 'rationed cloth to a 26 percent cut-back in the use of fabrics', calling for a more meagre use of cloth in the form of the 'streamlined suits by Uncle Sam' (Schoeffler and Gale 1973: 24). Indeed, as Cosgrove put it, 'The regulations effectively forbade the manufacture of Zoot suits' (Cosgrove 1989: 9). Malcolm X makes no direct reference to these social and political issues in his autobiography. Indirectly, the point is made when 'Harlem Red' (the nomenclature signalling his acceptance by Harlemites, that was to become his home) exploits his 'clown outfit' to 'tom fool' his way out of being drafted into the army and fight for Uncle Sam:

> I dragged out the wildest suit in New York. This was 1943. The day I went down there, I costumed like an actor. With my wild Zoot suit I wore the yellow knob-toe shoes, and I frizzed my hair up into a reddish bush of conk.
>
> (Malcolm X 1968: 193–4)

As mentioned above, in his later life the conk may have acquired connotations of denying one's 'Blackness', but in 1943 it was part of the visual symbols of Black self-fashioning, as part of a complete wardrobe that was part of an urban Black trend.

The Zoot suit was vehemently un-American, solely entrenched in African American or Mexican culture, therefore non-white. Effectively, in this stage of his life as a Zoot-suit-wearing youth from 1942 onwards, Malcolm was undoubtedly one of 'the stewards of something uncomfortable' (Ellison 1947: 381). Lee was perhaps right to launch into his biography of Malcolm X with a highly charged performance of ghetto adornments. The Zoot suit was not just about high-rolling, and hanging with the 'Homeboys', it was about the attainment of power and control of the self by the wearer. Here was Black Power some twenty-odd years before the official counter-discourse of the movement of the same name, tailored into a specific style of suit, an attitude in opposition to White Power constructed in the authoritarian and patriotric garments of the military uniform of the stream-lined, rationed suit. One could say that here, in the fabric and cut of three suits—the Zoot suit, the 'streamlined suit by Uncle Sam' and the military suit of the soldier—the social tension that has marred the texture of American society was played out in the public arena of the actual streets of America or the panoptic plane of the draft board.

Foucault, then, is useful in an attempt to understand the importance of dress in the life of Malcolm X as a political and cultural icon of this panoptic situation. Dress for Malcolm X not only provided and linked him with 'pleasure and individual freedom [in] the control over the self in one's regulated relations with others' (Lechte 1994: 114), but during his self-construction during his Zoot suit period, and most importantly coupled with the conk hairstyle, he was linked to the extended socio-political meanings of that subcultural dress. This was a successful technology of the self that doubled as a counter-discourse. Clothes then provide the instruments that empower the body to counteract a dominant ideology. . . .

Prior to his departure to Mecca, Malcolm X wore the conservative attire befitting a member of the Nation of Islam of a plain, single-breasted suit, shirt and tie and classic horn-rimmed glasses, part of the iconography that *is* Malcolm X. Meeting El-Hajj Malik El-Shabazz on the day he returned from his pilgrimage, Haley can only express the change in Malcolm X through his appearance:

> When the blue Oldsmobile stopped, and I got in, El-Hajj Malcolm, broadly beaming, wore a seersucker suit, the red hair needed a barber's attention, and he had grown a beard . . . There must have been fifty still and television photographers and reporters jockeying for position, up front, and the rest of the Skyline Ballroom was filling with Negro followers of Malcolm X, or his well-wishers, and the curious . . . They picked at his 'racist' image. 'I'm *not* a racist. I'm not condemning whites for being whites, but for their deeds. I condemn what whites collectively have

done to our people collectively.' He almost continually flashed about the room the ingratiating boyish smile. He would pick at the new reddish beard. They asked him about that, did he plan to keep it? He said he hadn't decided yet, he would have to see if he could get used to it or not.

(Malcolm X 1968: 38–9)

Malcolm's choice of casual presentation to address a press conference some two hours after arriving in the country was change indeed. In this instance he had marked his individuality and chronic desire for temporal and spiritual change, to dislocate himself from his recent past as Malcolm X, the Minister of New York Muslim Temple No. 7 of the Nation of Islam, into El-Hajj Malik El-Shabazz, the founder of two new organisations in June 1964: Muslim Mosque Inc. and the Organization of Afro-American Unity. The aesthetic codes for men of the Nation of Islam, in regard to the presentation of the public self, was to be immaculate and unassuming: clean-shaven, well-maintained hair, plain conservative suit, well-polished (not highly shined) shoes. Abjection is perhaps the best explanation of this ambiguous self-presentation:

the abject is above all the ambiguous, the in-between what defies boundaries, a composite resistant to unity. Hence, if the subject's identity derives from the unity of its objects, the abject is the threat of unassimilable non-unity; that is, ambiguity. Abjection, therefore, is fundamentally what disturbs identity, system and order.

(Lechte quoted in Warwick and Cavallaro 1998: xvi–xvii)

Could the ambiguity inherent in the identity of Malcolm X be based on his past personas and the new words being spoken, effectively changing much of what had gone before? As a member and leading figure of the Nation of Islam, his immaculate, business-like attire underscored his orthodox Muslim practices, and his stringent views on race and racism—

essentially a mistrust of 'the white devils' (Malcolm X 1968: 302). In the Hotel Theresa his views had become more inclusive, no longer the binary struggle between Blacks and whites, them and us. His clothing transmitted mixed messages of ease and control, the space for difference and creativity. In this very public presentation and production of his self, Malcolm had controlled how he would be visually represented in the media. His relaxed attire of unkempt hair, the nonchalant, decorated self in the 'blustered' ornamented feature of a seersucker suit, was indicative of the confidence Malcolm had in himself to be himself. The cotton summer suit is a respectable item of the male wardrobe, but not on equal terms as the woollen summer suit, as it is prone to crease and therefore unable to retain its shape and the smart appearance of the wearer. The aura of elegance is lost. Its ability to keep the wearer cool overrides such sartorial drawbacks (Roetzel 1999: 115–16). A prosaic reading of the seersucker suit would foreground its function as effective summer wear, due to its cool and lightweight properties. In the heated context of a press conference, where El-Hajj Malik El-Shabazz had to explain himself anew on religion, politics and physical appearance, the suit was not only a sign of a new Malcolm, relaxed yet in control of his future, but also the correct clothing in order to function in such artificially heated conditions. He kept his cool to be cool. In addition, looking cool in the face of the media, which can so easily show one 'looking like a fool' (Malcolm X: 418)[8] was of primary importance to the media-wary Malcolm X. It was significant that he should present himself in this way, unpolished and unconventional, voicing new opinions indeed, he was fully aware that he had 'an international image no amount of money could have bought' (Malcolm X 1968: 420), and he wanted to maintain his credibility as a representative in 'the American Black man's struggle'.

That ephemeral quality of cool is generally linked with urban lifestyles, the avant-garde, the unconventional. The exacted expression of cool that Malcolm possessed had the power to entice the generally apolitical, self-obsessed 'ghetto hustlers' and 'ghetto youths'—themselves, connoisseurs of cool—to political issues. After all, by 1964 Malcolm X had amassed such support from Black Americans that he was described as 'America's only negro who could stop a race riot—or start one' (Malcolm X 1968: 423). He was successful in the construction of a dressed image and a social and political standing, whilst his expressed empathy with his people, by 'being real' and keeping in touch with his origins, had paid off:

> The ghetto masses already had entrusted me with an image of leadership among them. I knew the ghetto instinctively extends that trust only to one who had demonstrated that he would never sell them out to the white man.
>
> (Malcolm X 1968: 424)

To be cool then, is not only what Gabriele Mentges defines as part of a modern form of self-construction predicated by street consciousness (Mentges 2000: 1), but in the case of Malcolm X, a modern way of political thinking and being, to combine the urban with the intellectual to result in a particular form of pride in being Black.

The goatee beard, though, was the fetishised marker of his particular transformation. The decision regarding whether he was or was not going to keep the beard had a profound spiritual meaning for Malcolm X and his experience of the Hajj:

> Standing on Mount Arafat had concluded the essential rites of being a pilgrim to Mecca. No one who missed it could consider himself a pilgrim. The *Ihram* had ended. We cast the traditional seven stones at the devil. Some had their hair and beards cut. I decided that I was going to let my beard remain. I wondered what my wife Betty, and our little daughters, were going to say when they saw me with a beard, when I got back to New York. New York seemed a million miles away.
>
> (Malcolm X 1968: 451)

Malcolm X kept the beard until his death in 1965.

The name Malcolm X was already known and unique in the public consciousness. To style himself in this new, easy liberated guise, was exacting a personal confirmation of this change in his life, on a course that was more inclusive of other people, of other ideas, political and personal. This relaxed, minimal image was not an original image, as the so-called 'Modernists', jazz artists and followers had perfected the look during the 1950s (Polhemus 1994: 38–9). The image was not far removed from the discreet style he had adopted and adapted when he was part of the Black Muslims. In this new phase of his dressed-self, the worldly undertones of his Muslim style so clearly suffused in the Arnold portrait was foregrounded. This style treatment to individualise the self, in the fine-tuning of El-Hajj Malik El-Shabazz, enabled Malcolm X to dissociate himself from the members of the Nation of Islam, break away from being a 'Zombie—like all the rest of them' (Parks 1990: 234). Newness in the form of a new self had taken centre-stage. This particular constellation of body, the self and dress provided the interface between new directions in his political and religious thinking in order to take care of and know the self.

The use of dress as metaphor for transformation, to present himself as El-Hajj Malik El-Shabazz, harked back to the edicts of street culture and philosophy of his time as a 'hustler' in Harlem, New York, 'that in order to get something you had to look as though you already had something' (Malcolm X 1968: 193). There at the Hotel Theresa amid people who knew him well (namely his wife and Alex Haley), and people who thought they knew him (America's press, and through their newspapers and television news articles, all America and beyond), Malcolm wanted to be accepted for who he was now. The conflation of the visual presentation of himself and the words he spoke, a transformed individual now stood in their presence:

My pilgrimage broadened my scope. It blessed me with a new insight. In two weeks in the Holy Land, I saw what I never had seen in thirty-nine years here in America. I saw *races*, all *colors*,—blue-eyed blondes to black-skinned Africans—in *true* brotherhood! In unity! Living as one!

Worshipping as one! No segregationists—no liberals . . .
In the past, yes, I have made sweeping indictments of
all white people. I never will be guilty of that again—as
I know now that some white people *are* truly sincere,
that some truly are capable of being brotherly toward a
black man. The true Islam has shown me that a blanket
indictment of all white people is as wrong as when whites
make blanket indictments against blacks.

(Malcolm X 1968: 479)

Here in this moment of unveiling a new self, Malcolm X had
attained the pride he had longed for.

Notes
8. Malcolm X explains in his autobiography that he was referencing
the damage that can be caused by hate if 'spread unchecked', as it was
in America at this time.

References

Arnold, Eve (1996) *In Retrospect*, London: Sinclair-Stevens.
Berger, M., Wallis, B. and Watson, S. (eds) (1995) *Constructing
    Masculinity*, London and New York: Routledge.
Clarke, Graham (1997) *The Photograph*, Oxford and New York: Oxford
    University Press.
Cosgrove, S. (1989) 'The Zoot suit and style warfare' in Angela
    McRobbie (ed.) *Zoot Suits and Second-hand Dresses: An Anthology of
    Fashion and Music*, London: Macmillan.
Davis, Thulani (1993) *Malcolm X: The Great Photographs*, New York:
    Stewart, Tabori & Chang.
Denzin, Norman K. (1989) *Interpretive Biography*, London/California/
    New Delhi: Sage.
Foucault, Michel (1988) *Technologies of the Self: A Seminar with Michel
    Foucault*, ed. L.H. Martin, H. Gurtman and P.H. Hutton, London:
    Tavistock.
hooks, bell (1990) *Yearning: Race, Gender and Cultural Politics*, Boston:
    South End Press.
———. (1994) *Outlaw Culture: Resisting Representations*, New York and
    London: Routledge.
Lechte, John (1994) *Fifty Key Contemporary Thinkers: from Structuralism
    to Postmodernity*, London and New York: Routledge.
Malcolm X (1968) *The Autobiography of Malcolm X. With the Assistance
    of Alex Haley*, London: Penguin.

Mentges, Gabriele (2000) 'Cold, coldness, coolness: remarks on the relationship of dress, body and technology', *Fashion Theory*, 4: 10.

Parks, Gordon (1990) *Gordon Parks: Voices in the Mirror. An Autobiography*, London/New York/Toronto/Sydney/Auckland: Doubleday.

Phillips, Adam (1994) *On Flirtation*, London and Boston: Faber & Faber.

Polhemus, Ted (1994) *Streetstyle: from Sidewalk to Catwalk*, New York: Thames & Hudson.

Roetzel, Bernhard (1999) *Gentleman: A Timeless Fashion*, London: Konemann UK Ltd.

Schoeffler, O.E. and Gale, W. (1973) *Esquire's Encyclopedia of 20th Century Men's Fashions*, New York: McGraw-Hill.

Steedman, Carolyn (1992) *Past Tenses: Essays on Writing, Autobiography and History*, London: River Oram.

Warwick, Alexandra and Cavallaro, Dani (1998) *Fashioning the Frame: Boundaries, Dress and the Body*, Oxford and New York: Berg.

White, Shane and White, Graham (1998) *Stylin': African American Expressive Culture from its Beginning to the Zoot Suit*, Ithaca, NY and London: Cornell University Press.

CELESTE MICHELLE CONDIT AND JOHN LOUIS LUCAITES ON THE LIMITS OF REVOLUTIONARY RHETORIC

The correlation between the recent revival of interest in Malcolm X among America's Black male youth and the Los Angeles riots of 1992 should not surprise us.[1] After all, the Los Angeles riots were (allegedly) precipitated by an inherently racist juridical system and a racist judicial decision. And it was Malcolm X, America's most thorough and relentless revolutionary dissident of the 1960s, who loudly implored his Black brothers and sisters to use "all means necessary" to bring about social and political justice and equality for Black America. Indeed it does not take much imagination to hear Malcolm X respond to the verdict in the Rodney King case in words similar to those used to express his outrage following the murder of four Black children in the bombing of the 16th St. Baptist Church in Birmingham, Alabama, only 2 weeks after the 1963 march on Washington:

It's time for Negroes to defend themselves . . . this doesn't mean forming rifle clubs and going out looking for people, but it is time, in 1964, if you are a man, to let that man [the White man] know. If he's not going to do his job in running the government and providing you and me with the protection that our taxes are supposed to be for, since he spends all those billions for his defense budget, he certainly can't begrudge you and me spending $12 or $15 for a single-shot or double-action. I hope you understand. Don't go out shooting people, but any time, brothers and sisters, and especially the men in this audience—some of you wearing Congressional Medals of Honor, with shoulders this wide, chests this big, muscles that big—any time you and I sit around and read where they bomb a church and murder in cold blood, not some grownups, but four little girls while they were praying to the same god the white man taught them to pray to, and you and I see the government go down and can't find who did it. . . . No, if you never see me another time in your life, if I die in the morning, I'll die saying one thing: the ballot or the bullet, the ballot or the bullet. (Malcolm X, 1965e, pp. 43–44).

The phrase "the ballot or the bullet" serves as the title for Malcolm X's most well-known speech, originally delivered on April 3, 1964, and subsequently presented on numerous occasions until the time of his assassination on February 21, 1965 (Benson, 1987, p. 319). It was one of his most militant statements, and for that reason it drew a great deal of attention from the White mass media and the White political establishment, which interpreted it as an appeal for the violent overthrow of the U.S. government. To reduce Malcolm X's dissidence to that one speech—let alone that one phrase—however, is to treat it as a static and simple (perhaps even simplistic) response to the circumstances confronting Black America in the 1960s. It is also to assume that his appeal for revolution was an appeal to use violence to tear apart the prevailing social and political structures of the United States of America. It was none of the above. Rather, "the ballot or the bullet" constitutes only a portion of one stage in the complex rhetorical development of his dissent from the American dream of equality, a dissent that ultimately entailed the rather peaceful goal of radically redrawing the ideological boundaries of American life to constitute a viable space for America's Black citizens.[2]

It is, of course, impossible to know whether or not Malcolm X's revolutionary vision would ever have produced a positive and peaceful program of political action capable of effectively organizing, motivating, and directing Black America against the system that oppressed it, for he was robbed of the opportunity to try at the age of 39. However, it was not only time that conspired against Malcolm X's efforts to effect a radically changed America, for he was also constrained by the inherent characteristics of revolutionary rhetoric itself, that is, the power of language to advance or restrict social and political change. To understand the successes and failures of Malcolm X's dissension, as well as the full relevance of his life and words for contemporary times, it is necessary that we examine the rhetorical dimensions of his dissent with some care. . . .

. . . Perhaps Malcolm X's most powerful rhetorical weapon was his recharacterization of Blacks through a revisionary Black history (see Lucaites & Condit, 1990). As part of this effort, he frequently disseminated scholarly findings about American slavery and about the African past, transforming the conventional White image of the African as a "savage" to that of a "king." So, for example, he would frequently note that "thousands of years ago the black man in Africa was living in palaces, the black man in Africa was wearing silk, the black man in Africa was cooking and seasoning his food, the black man in Africa has [sic] mastered the arts and the sciences . . . he knew the course of the stars and the universe before the man in Europe knew that the earth wasn't flat" (Lomax, 1968, p. 75). As Malcolm X later realized, by challenging the origins of the negative characterizations of Blacks constructed by White rhetoric, he actively revised the image of Africa and thus spurred the revision of a positive and affirming Black American

114

identity (Malcolm X, 1965b, p. 168; see also Malcolm X, 1970, pp. 160–161).

The vision articulated by Malcolm X that derived from Elijah Muhammad's myth was powerful. It dissented from 300 years of basic characterizations about the nature of Black Americans and their right to the American dream. Confirming the Black experience, it reversed the relationship between Blacks and Whites, casting "Whitey" as a crafty devil and Blacks as members of a noble and powerful race. This was without a doubt Malcolm X's most powerful and successful rhetoric with Black audiences, especially those living in America's urban ghettos, helping to convert thousands to the Nation of Islam in a relatively short period of time.

Elijah Muhammad's myth was also, however, a dissent that constructed great limitations for itself. Its authenticity came at the price of disengagement from this-worldly ways of thinking. It required a mythic consciousness that placed evidence and causality outside human time. It thereby removed the possibility for collective human action in the world. Indeed, Elijah Muhammad required his people to withdraw from political action. And it was in this context that an increasingly reluctant Malcolm X rearticulated the passive stance that left action to Allah alone: "But as God made Pharaoh's magicians bow before Moses, and the scribes and Pharisees bow before Jesus, He plans today to make all opposition, both at home and abroad, bow before the truth that is now being taught by the Honorable Elijah Muhammad" (Malcolm X, 1968/1991a, p. 119). Within the structure of this rhetoric, Malcolm X could take no action other than to warn of the new system, "which God Himself is preparing to establish" (Malcolm X, 1968/1991a, p. 117).

Perhaps the most telling inadequacy of the myth was the solution it proposed to the Black man's problem. Malcolm X argued that, until Allah acted, Whites should establish a separate nation for Blacks within the geographical boundaries of the United States of America by granting them the land contained by several established states. Social and political policies conceived solely through a mythic vision are typically doomed to failure, and this was clearly the case here. Such a proposal was only one short step removed from Marcus Garvey's appeals for pan-Africanism in the 1920s, and, as most of the Black speakers who argued against Malcolm X in debate during this period indicated, it was an altogether unrealistic solution to the problem of racial disharmony in America.

The dissent constructed by the Elijah Muhammad–Malcolm X myth was clearly more powerful and effective than that of Malcolm Little's earlier acting-out period. It provided real grounds for personal empowerment, both by establishing a historically grounded sense of selfhood and by building a tightly knit community that circulated Black economic resources among other Blacks. In important ways, however, it remained merely a reflection of White America's system of values. Black Muslims were not to smoke, drink, take drugs, or swear, but they worked hard in small business enterprises as well as on factory assembly lines, and their women were silent servants. Elijah Muhammad's vision reproduced capitalism and patriarchy, even as it mounted a challenge to White racism. Most important, the step out of the here and now that gave it the rhetorical space to revise the popular images of Blacks also left it powerless to act in the here and now. After a decade, the limitations of this dissent began to chafe on Malcolm X's fertile and active intellect, and it gradually led to a new stage in his rhetoric of dissent.

A DISSENTING RHETORIC: MALCOLM X SPEAKS OUT

In 1963, Malcolm X broke off his relationship with Elijah Muhammad and began his own Muslim ministry in New York City's Harlem. The breakup was precipitated by a number of different factors. In part, it was a function of Elijah Muhammad's growing envy over Malcolm X's public successes and his increasing popularity among the Black population. Additionally, and perhaps ultimately more important, it was a function of Malcolm X's increasing dissatisfaction with the limitations of the founding myth of the Nation of Islam, which undermined the opportunities for social and political activism. The most immediate cause for the rupture occurred in November 1963, when Elijah Muhammad censured Malcolm X for disobeying his orders to remain silent on the subject of President Kennedy's assassination. Not only did Malcolm X ignore these orders, but, in a question-and-answer period following a speech delivered in Manhattan, he referred to the assassination in insulting and potentially incendiary terms as "the chickens coming home to roost" (Malcolm X, 1971, p. 20). When it became apparent to Malcolm X that the censure was to be effectively permanent, he announced the creation of his own, independent Muslim Mosque, Inc., as a pulpit for a substantially new Black Islamic vision (see Malcolm X, 1965a, pp. 20–22).

This third phase of Malcolm X's dissent lasted from March 8, 1964, to his departure for Mecca 5 weeks later on April 13 and was dominated by appeals for "unity," "Black nationalism," and "human rights."[7] More specifically, he publicly characterized the shifting nature of his dissent as a new way of seeing, literally citing the capacity of a new generation of Blacks "to look at the thing not as they wish it were, but as it actually is" (Malcolm X, 1968/1991b, p. 135). The scales of Elijah Muhammad's myth of Islam had fallen from Malcolm X's eyes.

The vision of reality with which Malcolm X replaced Elijah Muhammad's myth did not entirely reject his prior rhetorical vision but transformed it to accommodate the world of experiences faced by America's Blacks. He thus substituted the story of White America's enslavement of Blacks for the story of Allah, recalling for his Black audiences that they had not come to America on the Mayflower but had been uprooted from their African homelands and brought to the "New World" in chains.[8] And when the slave ships on which they traveled arrived in the New World, they were forced to "pull plows like horses" and were "bought and sold from one plantation to the next like you sell chickens or like you sell a bag of potatoes" (Malcolm X, 1967, p. 65; see also 1965j, pp. 4–5). In one particularly trenchant rendition of the narrative, he would recall a book in which he had read that "George Washington exchanged a black man for a bag of molasses" (see Malcolm X, 1967, p. 65).

This slave narrative had been seared into Malcolm X's consciousness since the time of his prison readings. It was an extremely powerful narrative, especially for his primary audience, America's disaffected Black male youth, and he had employed it with effect from the very beginning of his ministry in the second stage of his dissent. Here, however, he shifted its rhetorical function, making it the central indictment of White America. It was no longer the devilish, genetic origin of Whites that constituted their evil, but their very actions. *Actual* sin replaced *original* sin, a point he frequently emphasized as he demonstrated that the enslavement of Blacks was not simply a matter of America's past, but was every bit as alive in 1963 as it had been in 1763. So, for example, he placed great emphasis on the "enslavement" perpetrated by the efforts of southern Dixiecrats to block the introduction of civil rights legislation in the halls of Congress, as well as the efforts of northern White politicians to gerrymander congressional districts in order to neutralize concentrations of Black voters (see Malcolm X, 1965e, pp. 28–30; 1965f, pp. 54–57; 1968/1991b, pp. 138–140).

In like manner, he transcended the standing Black Islamic demand for territorial statehood. At the press conference announcing the formation of the Moslem Mosque, Inc., he declared: "Separation back to Africa is still a long-range program, and while it is yet to materialize, 22 million of our people who are still here in America need better food, clothing, housing, education and jobs *right now*" (Malcolm X, 1965a, p. 20). The method he worked out for the "right now" was "Black nationalism." He characterized it in these terms:

> The political philosophy of black nationalism means that the black man should control the politics and the politicians of his own community. . . . The economic philosophy of black nationalism [means] that we should control the economy of our community. Why should white people be running the stores of our community? . . . The social philosophy of black nationalism only means that we have to get together and remove the evils, the vices, alcoholism, drug addiction and other evils that are

destroying the moral fiber of our community. (Malcolm X, 1965e, pp. 38–39)

In so doing, he transferred control of Black politics, economics, and morality from Allah and White America to a reconstituted community of socially and economically self-dependent Blacks. He founded this community, not in divine creation, but in an active, participatory understanding of the social and cultural roots of the Black world:

> We have to teach our people something about our cultural roots. We have to teach them something of their glorious civilizations before they were kidnapped by your grandfathers and brought over to this country. Once our people are taught about the glorious civilization that existed on the African continent, they won't any longer be ashamed of who they are. . . . The restoration of our cultural roots and history will restore dignity to the black people in this country. (Malcolm X, 1968/1991b, p. 142)

It was, therefore, especially important during this phase of his dissent that he stand for unity among Blacks. Indeed, this was the most clear-cut transformation from the earlier Malcolm X who had viciously attacked mainline civil rights leaders as Uncle Toms who had sold out their race in order to "drink some coffee—with a cracker" (Malcolm X, 1965d, p. 124). In forming the Moslem Mosque, Inc., he announced:

> I'm not out to fight other Negro leaders or organizations. We must find a common approach, a common solution, to a common problem. As of this minute, I've forgotten everything bad that the other leaders have said about me, and I pray they can also forget the many bad things I've said about them. (Malcolm X, 1965a, p. 20)

In spite of his new call for unity, Malcolm X still harbored major differences with other national Black leaders, such as Martin Luther King, Jr., and Bayard Rustin. Although he shared their commitments to equality, justice, freedom, and dignity, he refused to support the goals of integration and civil rights, and he adamantly repudiated the method of nonviolence. Malcolm X refused to abide the goal of "integration," for in his judgment it was predicated on the White supremacist assumption that Blacks ought to be integrated into White culture. This assumption was problematic on two counts. First, Malcolm X refused to believe that White America would actually allow such an integration to take place on anything like a level playing ground. Second, and perhaps more important, he believed that it denigrated the heritage of Black people, and thus their very being: to become valuable was to become a version of being White. As an alternative, he urged transcending the goal of "civil rights" with the goal of "human rights" and thus warranted his argument for equality on international values that exceeded the ideological boundaries and judicial authority of America's White-controlled government.

Finally, Malcolm X argued vehemently for "revolution," and as he repeatedly pointed out, revolutions, including the heralded American Revolution, are never "nonviolent." In his speech "A Declaration of Independence," delivered on December 4, 1963, he argued for the first time on a national level that Black Americans have the right to defend themselves if the White man's law fails to protect them:

> Concerning non-violence: it is criminal to teach a man not to defend himself when he is the constant victim of brutal attacks. It is legal and lawful to own a shotgun or a rifle. We believe in obeying the law.
>
> In areas where our people are the constant victims of brutality, and the government seems unable or unwilling to protect them, we should form rifle clubs that can be used to defend our lives and our property in times of emergency. . . . We should be peaceful, law abiding—but the time has come for the American Negro to fight back in self-defense whenever and wherever he is being unjustly and unlawfully attacked. (Malcolm X, 1965a, p. 22)

Malcolm X's new vision, born of his separation from Elijah Muhammad, was truly revolutionary, in the sense that it established the basis for a whole new way of thinking and talking about the relationship between Blacks and Whites. It was thus a revolution of identity, rather than a violent attempt to overthrow the prevailing social and political structures. In constituting this rhetorical revolution, Malcolm X went the distance by inaugurating the persona of a self-confident, Black identity that demanded all of the rights ever claimed by humanity. In the short run, this rhetoric was ineffective, for it seemed to ask for too much, too quickly, and in terms that were particularly threatening to the prevailing White political establishment. In the long run, however, it turned out to be Malcolm X's legacy to Black America. . . .

BEYOND DISSENT:
THE SEARCH FOR A CONSTRUCTIVE RHETORIC

In his *Autobiography*, Malcolm X credits his April 1964 trip to Mecca with having a radicalizing effect on his social and political vision. He recounts, for example, how the experience of sharing the Hajj with people of all colors convinced him of the possibility for a truly universal brotherhood (Malcolm X & Haley, 1966, pp. 318–342). When he returned to the United States from Mecca in May of that year, there was a marked and dramatic alteration in his rhetoric.

The most salient shift in Malcolm X's public discourse, at least from the perspective of White America, was his virtually complete abandonment of the claim that all Whites were inherently evil. The White media worked hard to treat this admission as a kind of absolution (see Capouya, 1965; Handler, 1964; "Malcolm X Makes Pilgrimage to Mecca," 1964; "Malcolm X Pleased by Whites' Attitudes on Trip To Mecca," 1964; "Malcolm X Woos Two Rights Leaders," 1964). However, Malcolm X was not about to let White America off the hook just because Whites in other parts of the world had learned to treat skin color as an accidental fact rather than a seigneurial emblem. Thus he noted:

In the past, yes, I have made sweeping indictments of *all* white people. I never will be guilty of that again—as I know now that some white people *are* truly sincere, that some truly are capable of being brotherly toward a black man ... [but] here in America, the seeds of racism are so deeply rooted in the white people collectively, their belief that they are "superior" in some way is so deeply rooted, that these things are in the national white subconsciousness. (Malcolm X & Haley, 1966, pp. 362–363)

As he explained it in an interview in the *Village Voice* (Malcolm X, 1965h, p. 213):

I haven't changed. I just see things on a broader scale. . . . If you attack [the White man] because he is white, you give him no out. He can't stop being white. We've got to give the man a chance. He probably won't take it, the snake. But we've got to give him a chance.

Although this shift did not give White America the absolution it sought, it thoroughly uprooted and transformed Malcolm X's previous rhetoric of dissent. No longer was "Black nationalism" an appropriate goal. As Malcolm X (1965g) put it in a 1965 television interview, "I believe in a society in which people can live like human beings on the basis of equality" (p. 197). He no longer supported a Black state or opposed the integration implicit in intermarriage. Although he still thought that liberal Whites could best help the cause by forming White consciousness-raising groups, he had to find a new path to achieving "equality," one that embraced neither King's nonviolent, humbling, identity-denying approach nor his own prior path toward a revised "separate but equal" doctrine. . . .

TOWARD CONSIDERATION OF THE LIMITS OF THE RHETORIC OF REVOLUTIONARY DISSENT

Malcolm X was the herald of the revolution of Black consciousness in the 1960s. He helped to give Black America the self-confidence to scare White America into negotiating with it (see Cone, 1991; Lucaites & Condit, 1990). The limits of that revolutionary rhetoric are all too clear today. Malcolm X did not change the racist underpinnings of America's economic structures, nor did he have a very direct impact on altering America's political system. These limits, however, can hardly be located in Malcolm X himself, for as a leader he stretched both his own thoughts and the vision of Black America far beyond the social and political horizons that had been publicly articulated prior to his expression of them. His inability to attract a large following derived as much as anything from the fact that he was so very far ahead of his people; they needed time, the time they would get upon his death, to catch up with him. . . .

. . . The limits of Malcolm X's revolutionary dissent were, therefore, limits willingly, if uncomfortably, self-imposed. They were limits inherent to rhetoric itself. A rhetor takes up the burden to persuade an audience, no matter how difficult the task, not to beat it into submission. Persuasion depends on the values and beliefs that exist or that can be reasonably constructed in conjunction with an audience. It also requires social and political negotiation, and it eschews the act of violence at all cost. A rhetor must, therefore, finally abjure a true revolution, which calls for an unfettered and absolute rejection of all that is, in favor of a torturous path through the constructive visions of what might be. This was the path that Malcolm X chose, and it is a path that those who today recall his appeals to "the ballot or the bullet" and to "all means necessary" as rallying cries for contemporary political action would do well to reconsider.

Notes

1. The revival of interest in Malcolm X has been motivated by a number of different events. The year 1990 marked the 25th anniversary of his assassination, leading to the establishment of the National Malcolm X Commemoration Commission and major features in the full range of national media, including the *New York Times* and the *Washington Post*, the nightly news programs of the major networks, and a *Sixty Minutes* update of Mike Wallace's documentary *The Hate That Hate Produced* (1959). Malcolm X has also been the subject of several popularly marketed books, including a biography

(Perry, 1991), a comprehensive comparison of his sociopolitical agenda with the sociopolitical agenda of Dr. Martin Luther King, Jr. (Cone, 1991), and the FBI files maintained on Malcolm X from 1953 until after his death (Carson, 1991). Finally, he has been a point of interest for filmmaker Spike Lee, who featured a dialogic relationship between Malcolm X and Dr. King in his 1990 movie Do *the Right Thing* and prepared a controversial film biography of Malcolm X released in 1992 just as this essay was going to press (see Fraser, 1990; Mills, 1990; Sterritt, 1991; Trescot, 1991).

2. The word *constitute* is used here to suggest the sense in which a rhetoric "positions the reader [or audience] towards political, social and economic action in the material and world" (see Charland, 1987, p. 141).

7. Four speeches unambiguously exemplify this period: "A Declaration of Independence, March 12, 1964"; the speech delivered at "The Leverett House Forum, March 18, 1964"; "The Ballot or The Bullet, April 3, 1964"; and "The Black Revolution, April 8, 1964." The similarities between the various audiences addressed by these speeches—White socialists, White academics, and largely Black audiences—suggest that, although Malcolm varied his tone to adapt to different groups, the substance of his message was remarkably consistent in this period.

8. This theme began to emerge in Malcolm X's public discourse as early as November 1963 (see Malcolm X, 1965j, pp. 5–6), but it flourished during this third period of dissent.

References

Benson, T. (1974). Rhetoric and autobiography: The case of Malcolm X. *Quarterly Journal of Speech*, 60, 1–13.

Benson, T. (1987). Malcolm X. In B. K. Duffy & H. R. Ryan (Eds.), *American orators of the twentieth century: Critical studies and sources* (pp. 317–322). Westport, CT: Greenwood.

Campbell, F. C. (1970). Voices of thunder, voices of rage: A symbolic analysis of a selection from Malcolm's speech, "Message to the Grass Roots." *Speech Teacher*, 19, 101–110.

Capouya, E. (1965, November 20). A brief return from Mecca. *Saturday Review*, pp. 42–44.

Carson, C. (1991). *Malcolm X: The FBI file.* New York: Carroll & Graf.

Charland, M. (1987). Constitutive rhetoric: The case of the *peuple québecois. Quarterly Journal of Speech*, 73, 133–150.

Clark, K. (1985). *King, Malcolm, Baldwin: Three interviews by Kenneth B. Clark.* Middletown, CT: Wesleyan University Press. (Original work published 1963)

Clasby, N. (1974). The autobiography of Malcolm X: A mythic paradigm. *Journal of Black Studies*, 5, 18–34.

Cone, J. H. (1991). *Martin and Malcolm and America: A dream or a nightmare*. Maryknoll, NY: Orbis.

Doty, W G. (1986). *Mythography: The study of myths and rituals*. University of Alabama Press.

Eakin, P J. (1976). Malcolm X and the limits of autobiography. *Criticism*, 3, 230–242.

Epps, A. (1972). The theme of exile in the Harvard speeches. In A. Epps (Ed.), *Malcolm X: Speeches at Harvard* (pp. 82–98). New York: Paragon House. (Original work published 1968)

Flick, H. (1980). A question of identity: Malcolm X's use of religious themes as a means for developing a Black identity. *Negro Educational Review*, 31, 140–149.

Flick, H. (1981). Malcolm X: The destroyer and creator of myths. *Journal of Black Studies*, 12, 166–178.

Flick, H., & Powell, L. (1988). Animal imagery in the rhetoric of Malcolm X. *Journal of Black Studies*, 18, 435–451.

Fraser, G. (1990, February 20). 25 years later, Malcolm X's voice is finding new audiences. *New York Times*, p. A8.

Goldman, P. (1982). Malcolm X: Witness for the prosecution. In J. H. Franklin & A. Meier (Eds.), *Black leaders of the twentieth century* (pp. 305–330). Urbana: University of Illinois Press.

Handler, M. S. (1964, October 4). Malcolm rejects racist doctrine: Also denounces Elijah [Muhammad] as a religious "faker." *New York Times*, p. 59.

The hate that hate produced. (1959). *Mike Wallace show*. Televised in New York City, July 9–13, 1959.

Illo, J. (1966). Rhetoric of Malcolm X. *Columbia University Forum*, 9, 5–12.

Lincoln, C. E. (1961). *The Black Muslims in America*. Boston: Beacon.

Lomax, L. E. (1963). *When the word is give: A report on Elijah Muhammad Malcolm X, and the Black Muslim world*. New York: New American Library.

Lomax, L. E. (1968). *To kill a Black man*. Los Angeles: Holloway House.

Lucaites, J. L., & Condit, C. M. (1990). Reconstructing <equality>: Culturetypal and counter-cultural rhetorics in the martyred Black vision. *Communication Monographs*, 57, 5–24.

Malcolm X (1965a). A declaration of independence, 12 March 1964. In G. Breitman (Ed.), *Malcolm X speaks* (pp. 18–22). New York: Grove.

Malcolm X (1965b). After the bombing, 14 February 1965. In G. Breitman (Ed.), *Malcolm X speaks* (pp. 157–177). New York: Grove.

Malcolm X (1965c). Answer to question, militant labor forum, 28 January 1965. In G. Breitman (Ed.), *Malcolm X speaks* (pp. 203–204). New York: Grove.

Malcolm X (1965d). At the Audubon, 11 November, 1964, 13 December 1964. In G. Breitman (Ed.), *Malcolm X speaks* (pp. 88–104 and 115–136). New York: Grove.

Malcolm X (1965e). The ballot or the bullet, 3 April 1964. In G. Breitman (Ed.), *Malcolm X speaks* (pp. 23–44). New York: Grove.

Malcolm X (1965f). The Black revolution, 8 April 1964. In G. Breitman (Ed.), *Malcolm X speaks* (pp. 45–57). New York: Grove.

Malcolm X (1965g). Interview on the Pierre Berton Show, taped at Station CFTO-TV in Toronto, 19 January 1965. In G. Breitman (Ed.), *Malcolm X speaks* (pp. 196–197). New York: Grove.

Malcolm X (1965h). Interview in the *Village Voice*, 25 February 1965. In G. Breitman (Ed.), *Malcolm X speaks* (p. 213). New York: Grove.

Malcolm X (1965i). Interview, Station WBAI-FM, 28 January 1965. In G. Breitman (Ed.), *Malcolm X speaks* (pp. 222–223). New York: Grove.

Malcolm X (1965j). Message to the grass roots, 9 November 1963. In G. Breitman (Ed.), *Malcolm X speaks* (pp. 3–19). New York: Grove.

Malcolm X (1965k). Rally for the Organization of Afro-American Unity in Harlem, 24 January 1965. In G. Breitman (Ed.), *Malcolm X speaks* (p. 201). New York: Grove.

Malcolm X (1965l). With Mrs. Fannie Lou Hamer, 20 December 1964. In G. Breitman (Ed.), *Malcolm X speaks* (pp. 105–114). New York: Grove.

Malcolm X (1967). A poor comparison, a response to a questioner following his presentation of "The Black Revolution," on 8 April 1964. In G. Breitman (Ed.), *Malcolm X on Afro-American history* (p. 65). New York: Pathfinder.

Malcolm X (1968). Interview with Stan Bernard. In L. Lomax, *To kill a Black man* (pp. 238–241). Los Angeles: Holloway House.

Malcolm X (1970). The *Young Socialist* interview (New York, January 18, 1965). In *By any means necessary: Speeches, interviews and a letter by Malcolm X* (pp. 157–167). New York: Pathfinder.

Malcolm X (1971). God's judgment of White America, December 4, 1963. In I. B. Karim (Ed.), *The end of White world supremacy: Four speeches by Malcolm X* (pp. 121–148). New York: Seaver.

Malcolm X (1991a). Speech to the Harvard law school forum, 24 March 1961. In A. Epps (Ed.), *Malcolm X: Speeches at Harvard* (pp. 115–130). New York: Paragon House. (Original work published 1968)

Malcolm X (1991b). The Leverett House forum of March 18, 1964. In A. Epps (Ed.), *Malcolm X: Speeches at Harvard* (pp. 131–160). New York: Paragon House. (Original work published 1968)

Malcolm X & Haley, A. (1966). *The autobiography of Malcolm X*. New York: Grove.

Malcolm X makes pilgrimage to Mecca: Describes new insights on race relations. (1964, May 8). *New York Times*, p. 1.

Malcolm X pleased by Whites' attitude on trip to Mecca. (1964, May 8). *New York Times*, pp. 1, 38.

Malcolm X woos two rights leaders; Asks "forgiveness" for past remarks and seeks unity. (1964, May 19). *New York Times*, p. 22.

Mills, D. (1990, February 25). The resurrection of Malcolm X; 25 years after his assassination, rekindled interest in the slain activist. *Washington Post*, p. 1.

Perry, B. (1991). *Malcolm: The life of a man who changed Black America*. New York: Station Hill.

Sterritt, D. (1991, September 12). Making a film of Malcolm X. *Christian Science Monitor*, p. 12.

Trescott, J. (1991, August 18). Battle of Malcolm X; Spike Lee vs. Amiri Baraka—Who should immortalize the man on film, and how? *Washington Post*, p. 61.

BASHIR M. EL-BESHTI ON IDENTITY AND THE AUTOBIOGRAPHICAL VOICE

The autobiography, as a genre, is characterized by what might be called "a double focus," a split between the identity of the person whose life is being recounted and the voice of the person recounting. In *The Autobiography of Malcolm X*, this double focus or split personality is most pronounced. There is Malcolm in all his various guises and transformations— Malcolm Little, Mascot, Homeboy, Detroit and Harlem Red, Satan—and Malcolm the authorial speaking voice, the one telling us about this string of provisional identities that finally culminate with the autobiographical self, one that is seen to be final and complete.

In terms of didacticism, *The Autobiography* depends on the narrative continuity between the younger Malcolm's experience and the fully-developed sensibility of Malcolm the autobiographer. The younger Malcolm spreads himself in discourse and it is left to the mature Malcolm to make modest disclaimers ("I was a zombie then").[1] Malcolm, the authorial voice, the mature, integrated human being, frequently interrupts the story being told to direct our attention to one didactic point or another. This can be tiresome, especially in the post-conversion chapters: we feel him to be directing our responses this way and that like a sheepdog—but without the interplay between him and his sensitive but limited younger self, the story's method and meaning could not be as powerful. For instance, Malcolm remembers that when he stopped eating pork in prison:

> It made me very proud, in some odd way. One of the universal images of the Negro, in prison and out, was that he couldn't do without pork. It made me feel good to see that my not eating it had especially startled the white convicts. . . . Later I would learn, when I had read and studied Islam a good deal, that, unconsciously, my first pre-Islamic submission had been manifested. I had experienced, for the fast time, the Muslim teaching, "If you will take one step towards Allah—Allah will take two steps towards you."(156)

The religious symbolism is not anything that the younger Malcolm, involved as he is, could have recognized at the time, but the older Malcolm, guided by his Islamic faith and newly found knowledge, is capable of interpreting the particular event within a totalizing ideology that is now applied to one's life retroactively. Such revisionism is a central feature of the autobiographical genre. As Ross Miller has pointed out, "the pose of the autobiographer as experienced man is particularly effective because we expect to hear from someone who has a completed sense of his own life and is therefore in a position to tell what he has discovered."[2]

The double focus of *The Autobiography*, the split personality of the subject, and hence the gap between what the mature Malcolm writes (or tells Haley) and what the young character says, gradually narrows down. As the historical moment catches up to the act of composition, as the narrative records more fully the growth of Malcolm's character, we see a fusion of speaking voice and the life that is being recounted. There is no real distinction between what is uttered in recollection and what is uttered on the page. Malcolm emerges from Mecca as a fully integrated human being: "In my thirty-nine years on this earth, the Holy City of Mecca had been the first time I had ever stood before the Creator of All and felt like a complete human being" (365).

In this sense, the progress of the autobiographical narrative—a continuum stretching from the historical moment up to the time of composition—becomes a progress towards a new identity. It is here that the autobiographical form intersects with the Bildungsroman; both give an account of the growth into maturity of an individual and hold out the possibility of education and of learning a new way. *The Autobiography*, however, is an interesting case of ruptured continuum and changing perspectives, of false starts and premature endings. Paul John Eakin has called attention to the fact that the bulk of the book had taken shape before the rift that occurred between Malcolm and Elijah Muhammad. He points out that Malcolm was to undergo a second conversion that brings to light the problematic of what Eakin calls "the autobiographical fiction of the completed self." Citing Alex Haley's apprehension that Malcolm might want to 'rewrite' the story in light of the split with the Nation of Islam and Malcolm's subsequent agreement with Haley's argument that a new perspective would rob the book of its suspense and drama, Eakin writes:

> At the end, then, Malcolm X came to reject the traditional autobiographical fiction that the life comes first, and then the writing of the life; that the life is in some sense complete and that the autobiographical process simply records the final achieved shape.[3]

The identity Malcolm assumes in Mecca, therefore, Eakin concludes, is far from being final and should be taken as "the last one in the series of roles that Malcolm X had variously assumed, lived out, and discarded."[4]

Malcolm, himself, seems to lend credence to the argument that the separation of life and life story is a fiction. In a letter to Haley, Malcolm laments: "How is it possible to write one's autobiography in a world so fast-changing as this?" (408). The statement seems to imply the recognition of the discontinuous nature of human identity and its social construction; it points to the shifting, protean, nature of the self, that one's identity is subject to and molded by the forces of history unfolding in time, and thus cannot be fixed. This, in turn, as Eakin has argued, points to the limits of autobiography; if the self cannot be fixed, is never complete, then the autobiographical narrative itself cannot sustain a definite shape.[5]

If that is, indeed, the conclusion Malcolm reached concerning the possibilities of the traditional autobiography, then the belief he expressed to Haley on more than one occasion that he would never live long enough to read the book in its finished form is all the more puzzling. The book could not have possibly attained proper closure while he was still alive. The rapidly changing circumstances of Malcolm's life would have made any ending both premature and obsolete. The fact that Malcolm pressed on with the project of writing his life, frequently urging Haley to proceed rapidly, without the possibility of real closure is perhaps a measure of his sense of impending doom, the sense that only death can put a violent and abrupt end to a self that is otherwise always incomplete. It would be left to Haley to close the book; autobiography gives way to biography. . . .

. . . Malcolm's Islamic beliefs, his belief in his own destiny prescribed by Almighty Allah, is the healing agent for a fractured narrative. It gives *The Autobiography* a continuous and definitive shape when the traditional paradigms of the genre fail it; a safety net, so to speak, that safeguards against the pitfalls of an ever-changing life. It does this by affecting the way the story is told, or, more precisely, the way Malcolm interprets his life story in autobiographical retrospection.

Islamic providentialism colors the way that Malcolm looks back on his own life. Every crisis that Malcolm faces, every step he takes that looks deleterious, every situation that seems insoluble, turns out not only for the best in the end but also a necessary step towards the fulfillment of his destiny. For instance, not only does Malcolm continually credit Allah for his numerous escapes from certain death—"I've so often thought that Allah was watching over me," (125) he says on one occasion—but even the humiliating loss to a white boy in a boxing match is seen as the work of Allah: "A lot of times in these later years since I became a Muslim, I've thought back to that fight and reflected that it was Allah's work to stop me" (24).

The net effect of the story being told from an overriding Islamic perspective is the sense that Malcolm is destined towards becoming a leader of black Americans. Even in his bleakest hour, lying on his cell bunk in prison, he would "picture myself talking to large crowds" (365). In retrospect, Malcolm accepts his life story as having been "written" by a higher force and hence the urge to record its meaningful content in an otherwise reluctant autobiographer:

> Today, when everything that I do has an urgency, I would not spend one hour in the preparation of a book which had the ambition to perhaps titillate some readers. But I am spending many hours because the full story is the best way that I know to have it seen, and understood, that I had sunk to the very bottom of the American white man's society when—soon now, in prison—I found Allah and the religion of Islam, and it completely transformed my life. (150)

Malcolm's story is, therefore, offered as a parable. It is important for Malcolm, however, to stress that he is not unique; he is a black man who shares his experience with other black men. If the notion of individuality is introduced, the justification for autobiography becomes more complicated: one has to reconcile the writing of one's life with the applicability of that life to the general condition of blacks. The later conception that humans are unitary beings deriving their essence from God complicates it even further: if we are all alike, then to preserve the peculiarities of an individual's life is, perhaps, not so pressing.

Malcolm skillfully manipulates the concept of selfhood, the remarkable details of his life, from the province of "abnormal psychology," as the editors of *The Saturday Evening Post* called it, to an Islamic ideal. He poses as a representative black man, a creature of a racist white society who had gone through all the phases a black man goes through in America. The phases that Malcolm goes through are many, but the spiritual hegira from ignorance, to enlightenment, and to salvation is basically an Islamic paradigm.[7] A fragmented individual, a wearer of what Ralph Ellison calls "masks" Malcolm saw himself as achieving full identity and integrity of the self in the religion of Islam. That is the sum of all experience in *The Autobiography*. His shifting perspective, after his visit to Mecca, on the nature of man does not frustrate the original aims of *The Autobiography*. Indeed, if we are all alike, then to read of one's life is to benefit from it.

James Boswell's rule of thumb when it came to writing the life of Samuel Johnson was that "the boy is the man in miniature: and that the distinguishing characteristics of each individual are the same, through the whole course of life."[8] Malcolm's distinguishing feature of course was his remarkable ability to continually transform himself. In this sense, the transformations are, paradoxically, the very signs of a stable core that can be solidified through time. But in following Boswell's account, which we may now link to Malcolm's belief that his life was written by God, we are forced to see the various transformations not merely as a series of disparate roles that Malcolm "had variously assumed, lived out, and discarded," but as gestalt, requisite and interconnected phases in the process of discovering the true and whole self ordained by God.

Malcolm might seem like a different man in each of his incarnations, but his essence—of fluidity, of emergence, of growth—always remains intact. Like a word traced by the science of philology that intrigued him so much, Malcolm's life "can lose its shape, but . . . keeps its identity" (416). In this we are also guided by the authority of Betty Shabazz, Malcolm's wife, who has written that "a lot of people say that Malcolm changed after the trip (to Mecca), but they never look at the totality and see that the man's entire scope had been broadened. They look at every individual change and say that Malcolm had changed from one thing to another."[9]

The broadening of the scope is intertwined with the act of reading and writing the self. In the process of discovering his true identity, Malcolm is always guided by the principle that "Allah always gives you signs, when you are with Him, that He is with you" (319). It is a small wonder that Malcolm warns his collaborator Alex Haley, "A writer is what I want, not an interpreter" (456). Malcolm saw the act of recording and interpreting Allah's signs towards the fulfillment of his destiny as one of his primary tasks as an autobiographer.

The signs come in rapid succession after Malcolm decides on the hajj: Ella financing his trip, his Muslim mates aboard the plane, the English-speaking party organized for his traveling benefit, the invitation to the cockpit by the 'dark' Egyptian pilot, driving in a car with the brother-in-law of the son of the ruler of Arabia (319, 320, 322, 324, 332). "Brother," Malcolm tells Haley, "I knew Allah was with me" (324). The whole Mecca episode is dramatized as the final beatific leg of a Dantesque journey towards salvation. In Mecca, Malcolm discovers both his Maker and his true identity—El-Hajj Malik El-Shabazz.

For the most part, however, the signs appear in the narrative in the form of moral crises, recollected sensations of anxiety and forced transformation that when joined together chart Malcolm's route towards salvation. Each moral crisis Malcolm undergoes not only culminates in the emergence of a new Malcolm, a transformed man, but also signals towards his final destiny. Even his career as a hustler, the phase in Malcolm's life that has received the most critical attention, can be construed, as Malcolm himself construed it, as a necessary step towards realizing that destiny.

By Malcolm's own account, the move to Boston which initiated his hustling career followed the infamous incident where Mr. Ostrowski, his English teacher, tells him "to be realistic about being a nigger" (36), in response to Malcolm's unrehearsed desire of wanting to be a lawyer. "It was then," Malcolm writes, "that I began to change—inside" (37). Again, the mature Malcolm praises Allah for the decision to leave Michigan and go to Boston, for "if I hadn't, I'd probably still be a brainwashed black Christian" (38).

If this sounds like a strange expression of gratitude considering the nature of his Boston experience, it also renders that experience a necessary step towards avoiding the fate of a "brainwashed black Christian." In Boston, and more so in Harlem, Malcolm is submerged in the hustling underworld of the ghetto, an inverted world order where his brother Reginald has to pose as a thief in order to sell his goods. But Malcolm soon learns that one of the real natural places where he can be black is the underworld: the contradiction is that in order to become a natural black, he must become a hustler. Malcolm feels he belongs (75)—the music, the dance are all symbolic of a natural rhythm, a medium of expressing a self long suppressed in Michigan. Malcolm's hustling energy, however, is cannibalistic as it feeds mostly on black victims. He paints a frightening picture of the Darwinian world, "truly the survival of only the fittest" (102).

The hustling underworld, nevertheless, afforded Malcolm a sense of community and racial pride: "Many times since, I have thought about it, and what it really meant. In one sense, we were huddled in there, bonded together in seeking security and warmth and comfort from one another, and we didn't know it" (90). But while Malcolm the protagonist could feel the enormously liberating sense of a newly found identity, it would take the maturity of Malcolm, the autobiographer, to recognize the pathological, even absurd, nature of that identity: "How ridiculous I was! Stupid enough to stand there simply lost in admiration of my hair now looking white" (54).

The conking of the hair, the white girlfriend, are signs of a psyche still dependent on the white ethic even as it ostensibly rebels against it. The syndrome is a familiar one: Malcolm recalls how his own father had favored him because "as anti-white as my father was, he was subconsciously so afflicted with the white man's brainwashing of Negroes that he inclined to favor the light ones, and I was his lightest child" (4). In more clinical terms, Frantz Fanon has called this psychological phenomenon the "affective erethism," by which he means, "a constant effort to run away from his (the black man's) own individuality, to annihilate his own presence."[10]

When Malcolm emerges from prison as the fiery Minister Malcolm X, proud of his blackness, confident of his superiority, conscious of his presence, the transformation seems complete. But as much as Malcolm would like for us to believe that his hustling days were over, that they belonged to an entirely different man, they still, nevertheless, form a large part of his working mentality. He knew, for instance, that he was being set up by the Nation of Islam after the announcement of his "silencing." "I hadn't hustled in the streets for years for nothing," (302) he proudly proclaims.

But Malcolm was also proud of the fact that he could talk with the 'middle class' Negro and with the ghetto hustler just as easily as he could talk with the faculty and students at Harvard (310). His hustling experience is what separates Malcolm, by his own reckoning, from the so-called downtown black leaders; without it, he would probably be one of the downtown black leaders himself or, worse, "a brainwashed black Christian."

The transformation from hustler to revolutionary is not totally surprising or inexplicable:

> The hustler, out there in the ghetto jungles, has less respect for the white power structure than any other Negro in North America. The ghetto hustler is internally restrained by nothing. He has no religion, no concept of morality, no civic responsibility, no fear—nothing. To survive, he is out there constantly preying upon others, probing for any human weakness like a ferret (311).

Malcolm's hustling days, although recounted with disgust and self denunciation, taught him to break all bonds, to lose all respect for racist white society—the very condition necessary to preach the racially rigid ideology of the Nation of Islam. . . .

. . . But the break with the Nation of Islam was inevitable from a moral as well as a political point of view. The perception of the Nation as "talk only" Muslims weighed heavily on Malcolm's soul. Here too, it pointed to the wide gulf between actions and values:

If I harbored any personal disappointment whatsoever, it was that privately I was convinced that our Nation of Islam could be an even greater force in the American black man's overall struggle—if we engaged in more action. (298)

Malcolm later conceived of an organization different from the Nation of Islam "in that it would embrace all faiths of black men, and it would carry into practice what the Nation of Islam had only preached" (315). In a desperate effort to regroup, he quickly announced the establishment of Muslim Mosque, Inc. But the name itself and the announced charter implies an act of political compensation; while the attempt to "incorporate" anxiously marks Malcolm's political agenda as a separate entity from that of Muhammad's, it reduces Islam to merely a medium of political exchange. In Malcolm's mind, Elijah Muhammad had robbed the Islam of the Nation from any serious and meaningful political weight and spiritual significance. One can compensate for the political vacuity of the Nation; moral guidance and vision, on the other hand, cannot be incorporated. Then came the signs and the trip to Mecca.

Malcolm, of course, walks into the world of "orthodox" Islam in its purest, most idealistic form. The hajj as a ritual dissolves, if only temporarily, the divisions, the internal strife, the barriers separating humans; in other words, the reality of the Muslim world. It is a leveller matched only by death. The Izar and the Rida, the clothes worn during the state of Ihram, however, eventually have to come off and when they do one can indeed tell a king from a peasant.

When Malcolm returns to his reality, it is not surprising that we find him struggling as to how to translate the ideal of "one god, one man" and the polyracial vision of the true Islam into a political program. "I'm man enough to tell you," Malcolm tells one reporter, "that I can't put my finger on exactly what my philosophy is now, but I'm flexible" (428). Malcolm is not talking about his religious philosophy; submission to God had secured him in his dignity and saved him from fear and despair, from guilt and confusion. In Mecca, he was "blessed by Allah with a new insight into the true religion of Islam, and a better understanding of America's entire racial dilemma" (339). Back in America, his newly formed Organization of Afro-American Unity [OAAU] and the ideology of Pan-Africanism are first attempts at a close political approximation of the moral vision of Islam. Malcolm of course was struck down by assassins' bullets while the OAAU was in its infancy; but it would be difficult to imagine that Malcolm would have remained static in the attempt to wed that vision to his basic mission of liberating the black man in America.

In the conclusion of the autobiography proper Malcolm clearly places that mission, his life and death, within the prophetic mode:

> I know that societies often have killed the people who have helped to change those societies. And if I can die having brought any light, having exposed any meaningful truth that will help to destroy the racist cancer that is malignant in the body of America—then, all of the credit is due to Allah. Only the mistakes have been mine. (382)

The turn on the conventional book dedication inevitably invites comparisons with the canceled original to Elijah Muhammad. In the original dedication Malcolm wrote:

> This book I dedicate to the Honorable Elijah Muhammad, who found me here in America in the muck and mire of the filthiest civilization and society on this earth, and pulled me out, cleaned me up, and stood me on my feet, and made me the man that I am today. (387)

While the original emphasizes what Muhammad had done for him personally, stressing the conversion itself as the turning point in his life, the conclusion of the book, on the other hand, looks forward to his death at the hands of a society he tried to cure as a divine gesture, a sign of his prophecy.

Notes

1. *The Autobiography of Malcolm X* (New York, 1984), p. 429. All further references are to this edition and will appear in the text.

2. Ross Miller. "Autobiography as Fact or Fiction: Franklin Adams, Malcolm X", *Centennial Review*, 16 (1972), p. 230.

3. Paul John Eakin, "Malcolm X and the Limits of Autobiography," *Criticism* 18, no. 3 (1976), pp. 241–242.

4. *Ibid.*, p. 231.

5. *Ibid.*, pp. 241–242.

7. See Abdelwahab M. Elmessiri, "Islam as Pastoral in the Life of Malcolm X", in John Henrik Clarke, ed. *Malcolm X: The Man and His Times* (New York, 1969), pp. 69–78.

8. James Boswell, *The Life of Samuel Johnson* (New York, 1968), p. 22.

9. Betty Shabazz, "Malcolm X as a Father and Husband", in John Henrik Clarke, ed. *Malcolm X: The Man and His Times*, p. 141.

10. Frantz Fanon, *Black Skin, White Masks*, trs. Charles Lam Markmann (New York, 1967), p. 60.

MARIA JOSEFINA SALDAÑA-PORTILLO ON MALE BLACK MUSLIM IDENTITY

Malcolm X begins his *Autobiography* with a scene of chaos and violence—his earliest memory—that serves as the narrative birth of the revolutionary:

> When my mother was pregnant with me, she told me later, a party of hooded Ku Klux Klan riders galloped up to our home in Omaha, Nebraska, one night. Surrounding the house, brandishing their shotguns and rifles, they shouted for my father to come out. My mother went to the front door and opened it. Standing where they could see her pregnant condition, she told them that she was alone with her three small children, and that my father was away, preaching, in Milwaukee. The Klansmen shouted threats and warnings at her that we had better get out of town because "the good Christian white people" were not going to stand for my father's "spreading trouble" among the "good" Negroes of Omaha with the "back to Africa" preachings of Marcus Garvey. (1)

The representation of Malcolm X in the discursive terms of Baker's religious man begins in this first passage. *In utero*, Malcolm X has been baptized by fire into the savage landscape of white Christianity, and into his messianic destiny. For Malcolm X, especially while under the tutelage of Elijah Muhammad, America is constructed as a doubly uncivilized space. White America is the territory of the devil. Within the uncivilized space of white America, there is another uncivilized space, the ghetto. The ghetto is a wilderness within the wilderness: its violence, poverty, and crimes are the cynical and intended results of white barbarity. In this opening passage, then, this structurally doubled wilderness portends the coming of Malcolm X. The Klansmen have hailed his father to the door—good Negro or messianic nationalist? Malcolm X prophetically comes forward, in his mother's womb, answering this call as a preordained revolutionary. The "back to Africa" preachings of his father and Marcus Garvey position Malcolm X for the reader as religious exile, as the latest in a long line of migratory black nationalists sent to interpret the wilderness for both black and white America.

The autobiography goes on to chronicle, in spectacular detail, the series of transformations that led to Malcolm X fully assuming the revolutionary subjectivity destined for him—orphan, ward of the state, star pupil, master hustler, degenerate prisoner, convert to Islam, Nation of Islam chief Minister, international black revolutionary. I would like to suggest, however, that this narrative of messianic transformation belies a condition of limited masculinity. Such a condition is multiply determined by the discursive, juridical, and material limits placed on the possibility of black male subjectivity in the racist United States of the 1940s and 1950s.[2] Malcolm X's transformation into a revolutionary subject is motivated by a desire not only for transcendence over this condition of limited masculinity, but also for the attainment of full masculinity defined as a unitary, self-determined, and determining consciousness. Indeed, the attainment of full masculinity represents the attainment of full humanity.

I. Black Masculinity as Excess

The fate of Earl Little, Malcolm X's father, makes evident to Malcolm X, at a very young age, the compromised nature of the masculinity available to black men in white America. The Ku Klux Klan, the Black Legion, and the police all punish Earl Little, not for any crime against white people, but rather for preaching self-determination and independence. Little is harassed as much for the kind of masculinity he practices as for the violation of a racial code—for having entrepreneurial aspirations and for daring to be independent as a black man. "As young as I was then, I knew," Malcolm tells us, "from what I overheard that my father was saying something that made him a 'tough' man" (6). These same acts of enunciation that constitute Earl Little as man—"tough," fearless—constitute "spreading trouble" for the Klansmen that visit Malcolm's mother. And once Little moved his family to Lansing, Michigan, the Black Legionnaires threaten Earl Little for being an "'uppity nigger' for wanting to own a store, [and] for living outside the Lansing Negro district" (3). Indeed, he is punished for appropriating the discursive terms of American consciousness: self-reliance, industry, mobility.

Eventually the Black Legionnaires burn down the Littles' house. The police and firemen, Malcolm remembers, do nothing to stop the fire or find the perpetrators. Instead, Malcolm tells us, the police begin to harass his father for having defended himself against the Black Legionnaires:

> After the fire, I remember that my father was called in and questioned about a permit for the pistol with which he had shot at the white men who set the fire. I remember that the police were always dropping by our house, shoving things around, "just checking" or "looking for a gun." The pistol they were looking for—which they never found, and for which they wouldn't issue a permit—was sewed up inside a pillow. My father's .22 rifle and his shotgun, though, were right out in the open; everyone had them for hunting birds and rabbits and other game. (4)

In these repeated visits to the Little home, the police are interested in the pistol as a sign of Earl Little's practice of masculinity. By shooting—in self-defense or in retaliation—at the white men who burned his home, Little goes beyond the bounds of acceptable black male behavior. Homi K. Bhabha has suggested that "colonial mimicry is the desire for a reformed, recognizable Other, as *a subject of a difference that is almost the same, but not quite*" ("Mimicry" 126). The police, as colonial subjects, fear that Little's mimicry has been too successful, that Little is the man they imagine themselves to be. He has acted as they would have acted, claiming the constitutional rights of self-defense and bearing arms. Little is no longer the Other as "the same, but not quite," but the Other as not quite not the same. Hence, the police must re-establish control in order to re-establish the difference between the partial presence of black manhood and the full presence of white manhood. Their arbitrary visits establish who has freedom and power and who does not. They are not concerned with what is evident, with what is permissible within the given terms of black manhood, the hunting rifles that "everyone had." They are obsessed with what Little might conceal, with the impermissible. The pistol becomes a trope for an essence, a secret full presence of manhood, "for which they wouldn't issue a permit," but which may lie hidden in Earl Little. It is precisely when Little ceases to be that which is self-evident to white men, when he ceases to be the transparent and authorized Other of mimicry, that the state must intervene.

The Black Legionnaires kill Earl Little when Malcolm is only six, making clear once and forever the consequences of exceeding the bounds of acceptable black masculinity. Thus, for Malcolm X, who understands himself as a black man laying claim to full masculinity, it is less an act of prophecy than a sense of history that leads him to tell us at the beginning of his narrative, "It has always been my belief that I, too, will die by violence. I have done all that I can to be prepared" (2). The murder of his father not only makes these limits viscerally clear, it also denies Malcolm *Little* a literal and figurative relationship to the patronymic. The murder of

Earl Little at the hands of contemporary white racists severs Malcolm Little from his father, symbolically replicating the racist violence of slavery which severs an entire race from its ancestry. Earl Little represents for Malcolm X not only his natural father. Little also represents an organic, patrilineal tie to a revolutionary consciousness and an ethnic, patrilineal tie to a prior civilization, both of which are generally the strict purview of white citizenship through the myths of the founding fathers and immigrant histories. Malcolm Little is severed from the patronymic, but Malcolm X re-establishes the mythic patronymic relationship in the narrative through the reconstruction of his father in black nationalist terms. Malcolm X, through *his* enunciatory act, fills the X, symbolizing the loss of a patronymic history, *with* a patronymic history of resistance, justice, courage, independence, and self-determination, characteristics generally reserved for the trope of (white) American subjectivity. . . .

II. Disciplining the Other and White Anxiety

In other autobiographies and testimonies of revolutionaries, guns formulaically serve as the trope of a fantasmatic full masculinity. As such, their possession and circulation recuperates that masculinity for the revolutionary. In Malcolm X's *Autobiography*, words or a certain mode of speech serve the tropic function usually reserved for weapons:

> Bimbi was the first Negro convict I'd known who didn't respond to "What'cha know, Daddy?" . . . [W]e would sit around, perhaps fifteen of us, and listen to Bimbi. Normally, white prisoners wouldn't think of listening to Negro prisoners' opinions on anything, but guards, even, would wander over close to hear Bimbi on any subject. . . . He liked to talk about historical events and figures. When he talked about the history of Concord, where I was to be transferred later, you would have thought he was hired by the Chamber of Commerce, and I wasn't the first inmate who had never heard of Thoreau until Bimbi expounded upon him. Bimbi was known as the library's best customer.

What fascinated me with him most of all was that he was the first man I had ever seen *command total respect . . . with his words.* (153–54, emphasis added)

To command the authority from blacks and whites that so impresses Malcolm X, Bimbi deploys a language that is pointedly not the vernacular of the hustler, but a language that lays claim to catalogued knowledge—historical, scientific, and literary. Bimbi's position of respect in the prison, his centrality to that community, is acquired through his use of this kind of knowing language. He inspires Malcolm X to take correspondence courses both in English and Latin. When Malcolm X converts to Islam, he proceeds obsessively to absorb this catalogued knowledge himself, first by copying the dictionary and then by reading the entire prison library.

Significantly, the "Saved" chapter that details Malcolm X's conversion to the presumably "Eastern" religion of Islam also details his mastery of a canonized, hegemonic form of Western knowledge. In fact, his submission to Islam and his mastery of Western knowledge are coterminous developments: "Mr. Muhammad, to whom I was writing daily, had no idea of what a new world had opened up to me through my efforts to document his teachings in books" (178). By literally retelling for pages all the things he learned on his quest for knowledge, this chapter provides the reader with an abbreviated history of the world, this time from the perspective of people of color in general and black people in particular. Malcolm X masters standard English in order to tell a significantly different story in distinctly similar terms: "I had to start telling the white man about himself to his face. I decided I could do this *by putting my name down to debate*" (184, emphasis added). The validity or absurdity of Muhammad's teachings is less important than the fact that Yacob's history of the human race provided the mythical framework for the reappropriation of black humanity in the terms of American discourse: a great past ordained by God with an imminently glorious future. Yacob's story provides a historical continuity denied black Americans in the hegemonic representation of the day. Malcolm X reverses Audre Lorde's theoretical premise (that has become a facile adage for many academics and activists) that the master's tools will never dismantle the master's house. In the NOI, Malcolm X disciplines the comic dissembling of "Sandwich Red" on the Yankee Clipper into an unflinching, historically documented denunciation of European civility, and he does this in a well-pressed suit.

This mastery of language provides Malcolm X with authority on a personal level as well. It is through the power of words that he reconstructs his personal patronymic at the beginning of the *Autobiography*, as he refuses the racist stereotyping that might label Earl Little a derelict father and instead inserts himself along with his father into the historical continuity of black nationalism. Minister Malcolm speaks with the authority of God and history, this time a Muslim God and a world history. Having reclaimed a past for himself and for black Americans through language, he can then proceed to reclaim the future by disciplining sexual boundaries in the service of the black nation.

What most impresses Malcolm X about the NOI, once he has been released from prison, is the responsibility it brings to bear on his brother Wilfred and the order that consequently reigns in the home:

Wilfred invited me to share his home, and gratefully I accepted. The warmth of a home and a family was a healing change from the prison cage for me. It would deeply move almost any newly freed convict, I think. But especially this Muslim home's atmosphere sent me often to my knees to praise Allah. . . . There was none of the morning confusion that exists in most homes. Wilfred, the father, the family protector and provider, was the first to rise. "The father prepares the way for his family," he said. He, then I, performed the morning ablutions. Next came Wilfred's wife, Ruth, and then their children, so that orderliness prevailed in the use of the bathroom. (193)

Wilfred then prepares the prayer rug on which the family, once purified, kneels together in prayer, facing East "in unity with the rest of our 725 million brothers and sisters in the entire Muslim world" (194). This daily ritualized performance of the prayer establishes order in the household. This is not just the order of a morning routine and who gets to use the bathroom first. Through this prayer ritual, gender categories are also performed, ritualized, and hierarchized; "the father prepares the way," the mother and children follow. Women cannot be expected to lead, protect, or provide for the family or the nation. Because, as Malcolm X tells us, these prayer rituals are performed in unity with 725 million people, these gender categories are elevated to a supranational level, even while they establish the NOI-as-family within the United States.

This description of Muslim prayer tells us far less about the performance of gender categories in the heterogeneous "Muslim world" than it tells us about the status of these categories and the romanticized nuclear family in the United States of the fifties and sixties. Malcolm X's recuperation of a normatively gendered and hierarchized family comes precisely at a moment when the myth of the white nuclear family is being challenged by sixties counterculture and particularly by the white counterculture. He sees the recuperation of the conventional family unit as essential for the survival and advancement of blacks in the ghettos of the United States. The recuperation of the family as model for black nationalist projects has now been soundly critiqued by African-American feminists and queer theorists.[11] The legitimacy of this criticism notwithstanding, Black Muslim recuperation of the nuclear family has the radical effect of inverting the logic of colonial mimicry. The construction of this family unit within the NOI, and Malcolm X's propagation of this family unit in the entire black community through his preaching, coincides with a growing anxiety among white Americans over the erosion of that family perceived as the foundation of the white nation. Indeed, the NOI success in the propagating of this idea of family produces this anxiety. Suddenly, Muslim black families appear to participate in this gendered, structured, and orderly family with greater success than all other families, black or white. Black Muslims live out the myth of the nuclear American family, "only more so."[12] This rationalized and disciplined unit of economic and ideological reproduction is no longer essentially white.

Finally, Minister Malcolm disciplines the hustling society into an industrious society. This was at the heart of the redemptive ministry of Malcolm X and the NOI. Malcolm X, as a member of the NOI, achieves the independence and self-reliance for the black man that his father desired. At various points in the *Autobiography*, he tells the reader that the NOI had its own newspaper, banking system, farms, processing plants, trucking business, chain of stores and restaurants. In the post–War World II politics of the late 1950s and early 1960s, the U.S. government was a major proponent of the modernization paradigm, of "self-sustained growth" schemes for Third World countries struggling for statehood. This teleological modernization paradigm—with the founding of the World Bank, the International Monetary Fund, and the proliferation of development projects—emerged as a method of maintaining colonial surveillance, political influence, and economic control over countries on the verge of national independence. As a refiguration of the logic of colonial appropriation, "development" held the promise of equal citizenship in the fraternal order of First World nations. Precisely as the First World, led by the U.S., was busy propagating this modernization paradigm all over the globe, the black brothers and sisters of the NOI were busy at home creating a modernized Muslim nation within a nation.

The NOI, in establishing this economic organization, adhered to the classic liberal formula for modernization. W.W. Rostow, chief architect of modernization theory for the United States, argues that development hinges primarily on a choice, on a community making the ethical choice of taking money out of the hands of those spending it on "prodigal living" and transferring it into the hands of those who will amass and invest it as capital (Rostow 24). The NOI, with its strict moral code, does precisely this. Money previously spent by converts on entertainment is centralized through donations to the mosques and funneled by the ministers, who function as an executive board, into Muslim businesses. Profits are "plowed back" into related businesses, jobs for Muslim brothers and sisters are created, wages grow, demand increases, the economy diversifies. Although Minister Malcolm saw his role as primarily spiritual, he played no small part in the NOI's economic efforts. He provided the converts. He fished for converts not only among the working blacks, but also among the drug addicts, hustlers, and prostitutes. Malcolm X sought to discipline the prodigal son into the industrious father, thereby appropriating the terms of the emerging post–W.W. II discourse of development. The NOI thus becomes a textbook case of the modern nation and demands equal standing with another modern nation, the U.S.[13]

I have suggested that Malcolm X as a Minister of NOI successfully recuperates the discursive terms of full masculinity for himself: mastery of language; the myth of family—both nuclear and national—with a clearly demarcated role for him as both father and minister; industry and self-reliance. Through the apparent recuperation of these terms, Malcolm X attains the fantasy of coherence that Judith Butler has suggested is at the center of *all* identity formation, and that I have suggested motivates Malcolm X in the quest for full subjectification:

> According to the understanding of identification as an enacted fantasy or incorporation, however, it is clear that coherence is desired, wished for, idealized, and that this idealization is an effect of a corporeal signification. In other words, acts, gestures, and desire produce the effect of an internal core or substance, but produce this on the surface of the body, through the play of signifying absences that suggest, but never reveal, the organizing principle of identity as a cause. Such acts, gestures, enactments, generally construed, are performative in the sense that the essence or identity that they otherwise purport to express are fabrications manufactured and sustained through corporeal signs and other discursive means. (Butler 136)

Through his words, acts, gestures, and desire, Malcolm X performs the coherence, "the organizing principle of identity as a cause," of the tropic American subject. He performs this tropic American subjectivity as an "inappropriate" subject, not only because he is black, but also because he is Muslim. In his performance of this subjectivity, full masculinity necessarily appears as hyper-masculinity, precisely because it is performed by a black man, an inappropriate subject. Malcolm X is at times indeed perceived as caricature. At the same time, when Malcolm X brings discipline to bear on this "hyper-masculinity," when he successfully usurps the disciplining function of the white state, he destroys for the white community the boundary between the white, Christian subject and the black, Muslim other. Butler suggests, "What constitutes through division the 'inner' and 'outer' worlds of the subject is a border and boundary tenuously maintained for the purposes of social regulation and control" (133). Malcolm X, as inappropriate subject, lays claim to the inner world of the (white) tropic American subject, thereby erasing that tenuous border. Thus he threatens the social regulation of the segregated U.S. of the 1950s and 1960s, not by armed insurrection, nor even by the peaceful means of non-violence, but simply by the enactment of a disciplined American masculinity, which lends him the appearance of being. This performance is a parody, a mockery, not because Malcolm X is parodic, but because Malcolm X in his recuperation of full masculinity as tropic American subject reveals to white men that they lack an original claim to this masculinity, this "internal core." Malcolm X reveals that there is no (white) essence to this tropic American subjectivity, because this subjectivity is a *fabrication* he can successfully represent. Therein lies the violation, the "violence" of Malcolm X, a gentle man who was never personally associated with physical violence. At the time of his death, all he had on him by way of defense was a pen that sprayed mace. But Malcolm X does violence in discursive terms.

Notes

2. The lynchings of black men in the South during these two decades are the most profound examples of how these multiple limits on black masculinity overlap. On August 28, 1955, Emmett Till

allegedly "whistled at a white woman." For exceeding the bounds of permissible black male sexual behavior, for transgressing the discursive sexual order, this fourteen-year-old boy was lynched, the material "check" on his masculinity in place even before he is a "man" in age. As juridical sanction of this policing of black masculinity, an all white jury acquitted the two white men accused of lynching the boy (Coe).

11. For a feminist critique of the deployment of a conventional family as model for the African-American community, see Spillers.

12. In the end, it is Elijah Muhammad's failure to conform to the highly moralized and gendered category of the patriarch that so deeply troubles Malcolm X, leading Muhammad to perceive him as dangerous to the NOI.

13. Malcolm X's attempt to bring charges of human rights violations on behalf of black Americans against the U.S. in the United Nations precisely threatened the U.S.'s claim to modernization and its attendant civil discourse. Such charges would inscribe the U.S. in the "barbarity" of the "underdeveloped" world that it set itself against. Also, if the U.S. government was not even going to treat its own self-reliant Muslim citizens as equal, then certainly it would not treat self-reliant nations as equal.

Works Cited

Acuña, Rodolfo. *Occupied America: A History of Chicanos*. 3rd ed. New York: Harper, 1988.

Baker, Jr., Houston A. *Blues, Ideology, and Afro-American Literature*. Chicago: U of Chicago P, 1984.

Bhabha, Homi. "Of Mimicry and Man: The Ambivalence of Colonial Discourse." *October* 28 (1984): 125–33.

———. "Sly Civility." *October* 34 (1985): 71–80.

Breitman, George. *The Last Year of Malcolm X: The Evolution of a Revolutionary*. New York: Merit, 1967.

Breitman, George, ed. *Malcolm X Speaks: Selected Speeches and Statements*. 1965. New York: Grove, 1990.

Butler, Judith. *Gender Trouble*. New York: Routledge, 1990.

Carson, Clayborne. *Malcolm X: The FBI File*. Ed. David Gallen. New York: Carroll, 1991.

———. *Malcolm X: The FBI File*. New York: Carroll, 1991.

Clark, Steve. *Malcolm X: February 1965, The Last Speeches*. New York: Pathfinder, 1992.

Clarke, John Henrik, ed. *Malcolm X: The Man and His Times*. Toronto: Macmillan, 1969.

Coe, Sue, with Judith Moore and Francoise Mouly. *X: For Malcolm X and all those who have been Xed out of the American Dream*. New York: New Press, 1992.

Collins, Patricia Hill. "Learning to Think for Ourselves," Wood 59–85.

———. "The Social Construction of Black Feminist Thought." *Signs: Journal of Women in Culture and Society* 14.4 (1989): 745–73.

Karim, Benjamin, with Peter Skutches and David Gallen. *Remembering Malcolm: The story of Malcolm X from inside the Muslim mosque by his assistant minister Benjamin Karim.* New York: Carroll, 1992.

Kelley, Robin D.G. "The Riddle of the Zoot: Malcolm Little and Black Cultural Politics During World War II," Wood 155–82.

Malcolm X. *The Autobiography of Malcolm X as told to Alex Haley.* New York: Ballantine, 1984.

Morrison, Toni. "Rootedness: The Ancestor as Foundation." *Black Woman Writers (1950–1980).* Ed. Mari Evans. New York: Anchor, 1984. 339–45.

Perry, Bruce. *Malcolm: The Life of a Man Who Changed Black America.* Barrytown: Station Hill, 1991.

Retamar, Roberto Fernández. "Caliban: Notes Towards a Discussion of Culture in Our America." Trans. Lynn Garafola, David Arthur McMurray, and Robert Márquez. *Massachusetts Review* 15 (1974): 7–72.

Rostow, W.W. *Stages of Growth: A Non-Communist Manifesto.* Cambridge: Cambridge UP, 1960.

Spillers, Hortence J. "Mama's Baby, Papa's Maybe: An American Grammar Book." *Diacritics* 17.2 (1987): 65–81.

West, Cornel. "Malcolm X and Black Rage," Wood 48–58.

Wood, Joe, ed. *Malcolm X: In Our Own Image.* New York: St. Martin's, 1992.

ROBIN D.G. KELLEY ON MALCOLM X'S RELATIONSHIP TO THE BLACK MIDDLE CLASS

The Die Is Caste

Unlike most black leaders prior to the early 1960s, including black working-class heroes such as A. Philip Randolph or Paul Robeson, Malcolm consistently identified with ordinary black working people and those displaced by the economy. He spoke their language and told their jokes. His was not simply another Horatio Alger story of how he rose out of poverty to become a hero. (And despite dozens of opportunities, he never sought wealth, leaving his family virtually penniless.) Rather, he invoked his experiences as an urban kid, former criminal,

150

man of the streets, to show his audience that he knows where they are coming from and never forgot where he came from. In fact, he so depended on this identification with poor black folk—particularly the young—that he exaggerated his criminal exploits, his poverty, and his urban upbringing.[4]

At the same time, Malcolm always had a love/hate relationship with the black bourgeoisie, though like most unconsummated relationships hate eventually became the dominant emotion. Even as a child in Lansing, Michigan, the sons and daughters of the black elite turned their noses up at the skinny red-head from that awful Little family. He was not only poor, but he was practically an orphan; his father was dead, and his mother had been committed to a mental institution. But he soon learned that these Negroes were nothing. He got his first real taste of black bourgeois pretentiousness when he moved to Boston with his half-sister Ella Little in 1941.[5]. . .

. . . As he grew less and less tolerant of the Hill crowd, Malcolm began hanging out in the poorer sections of Roxbury where he "felt more relaxed among Negroes who were being their natural selves and not putting on airs."[10] His newfound friend, Shorty, introduced him to the cool world of the zoot suit, the conk (straightened) hairstyle, and the lindy hoppers who spent their weekend nights at Boston's Roseland State Ballroom. When Malcolm donned his very first zoot suit, he realized immediately that the wild sky-blue outfit, the baggy punjab pants tapered to the ankles, the matching hat, gold watch chain, and monogrammed belt was more than a suit of clothes. It was a ticket into the "in crowd," a new identity that symbolized an increasingly militant and ultramasculine black street culture. The language and culture of the zoot suiters enabled Malcolm to reject white racism and patriotism, the rural folkways (for many, the "parent culture") that still survived in most black urban households, and the petit bourgeois attitudes of his "snooty" middle-class neighbors on the Hill. He found in the Roseland State Ballroom, and later in Harlem's Savoy, spaces of leisure and pleasure free of the bourgeois pretensions of "better class Negroes." For young Malcolm, his new world embodied the "true" black experience:

151

"I couldn't wait for eight o'clock to get home to eat out of those soul-food pots of Ella's, then get dressed in my zoot and head for some of my friends' places in town, to lindy-hop and get high, or something, for relief from those Hill clowns."[11]

Malcolm and his partners did not seem very "political" at the time, but they dodged the draft so as not to lose their lives over a "white man's war," and they avoided wage work whenever possible. His search for leisure and pleasure took him to Harlem where petty hustling, drug dealing, pimping, gambling, and exploiting women became his primary source of income. In 1946 his luck ran out; he was arrested for burglary and sentenced to ten years in prison. . . .

Varieties of House Negroes

When it came to attacking and ridiculing the black bourgeoisie, Malcolm was perhaps the least charitable of the NOI leadership. He called them "house slaves," "Uncle Toms," "Nincompoops with Ph.D.s," "Quislings," "sell-outs," and, of course, "bourgeois Negroes." And all of these terms did not necessarily mean the same thing. Malcolm essentially spoke of the black middle class in several different contexts and placed them in different categories. First, there was the elite he knew as a teenager: working-class black folk with upper-class pretensions. By trying to adopt the mannerisms of the authentic bourgeoisie, these nouveau riche (without the wealth!) carved out for themselves a whole black elite culture. Second, there were the truly wealthy blacks whose social and cultural lives were inseparable from that of the white elite. He excoriated this class for having little interest or tolerance for the masses of black people. And, finally, there were the self-proclaimed black leaders, the "handkerchief heads" who ran integrationist organizations and begged for Civil Rights.

In Malcolm's view, all three categories of the black bourgeoisie shared a common disdain for the culture of the black masses. Indeed, Malcolm usually identified the black bourgeoisie by its culture rather than its income or occupation. His experience with the "Hill Negroes" demonstrated that wealth wasn't the main factor distinguishing the black bourgeoisie from the rest;

it was their attitude, their adoration of European culture, and their distance from anything identified with ghetto blacks that rendered them elites. "They prided themselves on being incomparably more 'cultured,' 'cultivated,' 'dignified,' and better off than their black brethren down in the ghetto, which was no further away than you could throw a rock. Under the pitiful misapprehension that it would make them 'better,' these Hill Negroes were breaking their backs trying to imitate white people."[16] In a speech before a predominantly white college audience, he characterized the black bourgeoisie by its dress and mannerisms. "Uncle Tom wears a top hat. He's sharp. He dresses just like you do. He speaks the same phraseology, the same language. He tries to speak better than you do." More than anything, the black bourgeoisie are "ashamed of black, and don't want to be identified with black or as being black." Integration and intermarrying enables them to escape their black identity, which is why well-off black men are so anxious to marry white women and move into white neighborhoods.[17]. . .

. . . Depending on when you caught him, Malcolm characterized middle-class African Americans as either ignorant of their true selves and thus potentially transformable, or ineluctably exploitative and hopeless. Although self-transformation was crucial to Malcolm's life and ideology, he frequently implied that the black bourgeoisie was incapable of siding with the masses and giving up their class interests—what African revolutionary Amilcar Cabral described as "committing class suicide."[27] After his English teacher, the infamous Mr. Ostrowski, told Malcolm that his aspiration to become a lawyer was "no realistic goal for a nigger," he pondered what his future might have been like if he had been encouraged to pursue a career in law. He was convinced that if he had joined the black elite he would have been destined to become a turncoat: "I would today probably be among some city's professional black bourgeoisie, sipping cocktails and palming myself off as a community spokesman for and leader of the suffering black masses, while my primary concern would be to grab a few more crumbs from the groaning board of the two-faced whites with whom they're begging to 'integrate.' "[28] By making this statement, however, Malcolm was not only arguing that the bourgeoisie was hopelessly bankrupt; he was making a case for the primacy of experience. "All praise due to Allah that I went to Boston when I did. If I hadn't, I'd probably still be a brainwashed black Christian." While his gratitude to Allah offers a hint of fatalism, he is nonetheless suggesting that his experience with "ordinary Negroes" shaped his outlook and direction. He took a trip to Hell, no doubt, and even looked the devil in the face. But if he hadn't taken that horrible trip, he implies, he might have ended up with a fate worse than death—Malcolm Little, Esq.

I seriously doubt Malcolm believed that a formal education and a career in law would have corrupted him, however. On the contrary, he probably spent most of his adult life regretful for not pursuing his educational goals. Every time he looked into the eyes of his own attorney, black radical Conrad Lynn, perhaps he saw himself. He fashioned himself as an intellectual and spent many mornings at a Harlem coffee shop called 22 West on 135th St. engaged in lively debates with the same "Uncle Toms" he talked about so badly on stage and in the press. In speech after speech, despite his ravings against "nincompoops with Ph.D.s," he strongly suggested that as black folks became more educated, they would inevitably undermine the status quo. In a speech delivered at Harvard Law School in 1960, he argued: "Once the slave has his master's education, the slave wants to be like his master, wants to share his master's property, and even wants to exercise the same privileges as his master even while he is yet in his master's house." He warned Harvard's faculty and administration that "the same Negro students you are turning out today will soon be demanding the same things you now hear being demanded by Mr. Muhammad and the Black Muslims." Thus education, even in the white Ivy League institutions, was seen as potentially emancipatory—that is, as long as it is not limited to the sons and daughters of the elite. Real freedom depends on the poor, downtrodden masses gaining access to the master's knowledge.[29]

It was an incredible speech, for it reveals Malcolm's own envy and appreciation for formal education. Indeed, Malcolm not only showed an enormous amount of respect and admiration for institutions of higher learning, but he suggested that black intellectuals—if properly united—have the capacity to lead African Americans "out of this maze of misery and want." "They possess the academic know-how," he asserted, "great amounts of technical skills . . . but they can't use it for the benefit of their own kind simply because they themselves are also disunited. If these intellectuals and professional so-called Negroes would unite, not only Harlem would benefit, but it will benefit our people all over the world."[30]. . .

. . . So it is not wealth, per se, that renders the black bourgeoisie useless. It is their station in the Big House and their unwillingness to walk out. Unlike their ancestors, they have failed to live up to their responsibility to assist the downtrodden, to (as one middle-class black women's organization put it) lift as they climb. "The wealthy, educated Black bourgeoisie," Malcolm told a University of California audience in 1963, "those uppity Negroes who do escape, never reach back and pull the rest of our people out with them. The Black masses remain trapped in the slums."[34]

In fact, one of the less talked about reasons why Malcolm left the Nation has to do with the fact that NOI leaders began to look more and more like the greedy, wealthy Negroes he criticized. With disdain and sadness, he watched efforts at self-reliance and economic self-help through the establishment of businesses tragically turn into a private empire for the Messenger and his cronies. By the eve of Malcolm's break, the NOI had become a cross between a black mafia and a legitimate bourgeois enterprise. At one point, the NOI boasted of one of the most successful black-run financial empires in the country, with assets reportedly reaching 45 million dollars. With Elijah and his family riding around in chauffeur-driven Cadillacs and living in mansions, the Messenger began to resemble the very black bourgeoisie whom Malcolm hated. And Malcolm was well aware of the unscrupulous ways the NOI took its members' money, which included the outright misappropriation of funds. Benjamin Karim remembers one run-in between Malcolm and John Ali over thirty or forty thousand dollars New York's Temple No. 7 had raised to build a new mosque. When Malcolm asked about the money, Ali couldn't exactly account for it; he derisively said it had been invested in some other venture but couldn't say which one. Karim, who had never seen Malcolm so angry, heard him grumble something like, "They probably needed some loose change to dress Ethel [Elijah's daughter who was married to Supreme Captain Raymond Sharrief] up in diamonds and mink for a fancy night on the town."[35]

Ironically, the "house niggas" for whom Malcolm reserved most of his venom turned out to be some of the same people with whom he sought to build an alliance: traditional black political leaders and the Civil Rights establishment. His relationship to other black leaders, in Harlem and elsewhere, was never cut and dried. On the one hand, the Nation of Islam maintained rules against political participation—a policy Malcolm clearly disagreed with. He not only believed that political mobilization was indispensable but occasionally defied the rule by supporting boycotts and other forms of protest. On the other hand, Elijah Muhammad was always open to alliances with traditional black leaders and maintained cordial relations whenever possible. In July 1958, for example, African-American politicians hosted a two-day "Unity Feast" for Elijah Muhammad in Harlem where he was greeted by Manhattan borough president Hulan Jack, City Councilman Earl Brown, and columnist J.A. Rogers, to name a few. And at a Muslim-sponsored Leadership Conference in Harlem less than two years later, several prominent black leaders showed up, including Adam Clayton Powell, Jr. Malcolm even offered his guests bittersweet praise when he thanked black leaders in attendance for "at last catching up with the progressive thinking of the enlightened Negro masses."[36]. . .

. . . In some respects, Malcolm's dilemma was—and still is—inescapable. To escape it requires a remarkable analytical leap that would undermine the fragile basis upon which his conception of black nationalism was built. Like today's young nationalists weighed down by X caps and red, black and green medallions, Malcolm saw the black bourgeoisie as both enemies and misguided souls, sellouts and brainwashed Negroes who simply need a wake-up call from the Motherland. Few are willing to say, in no uncertain terms, that the black poor and the bourgeoisie have mutually exclusive interests.[45] For to do so would be to call into question the whole basis of nationalism, particularly a nationalism based on racial and cultural affinity. Even more damaging, however, is that it would close off any possibility of achieving individual success. After all, what are these young Soul Rebels striving for anyway? How can anyone expect young people coming up today to completely repudiate the black bourgeoisie, or any bourgeoisie, if contemporary Malcolmites are giving graduation speeches about the importance of getting paid or obtaining that degree "by any means necessary"?

Yet, Malcolm's reputation as a militant is partly built on his denunciation of the "house nigga." His current resurrection has a lot to do with growing class tensions between a successful, suburban, and increasingly disinterested black middle class and the so-called "underclass" left to rot in the slums. The word "bourgeois" has even become common lingo among Hip Hop artists and their fans to refer to black-owned radio stations and, more generally, middle-class African Americans who exhibit disgust or indifference toward young, working-class blacks. For Ice T, living in the lap of luxury is not what renders the black bourgeoisie bankrupt, but rather their inability to understand the world of the ghetto. In an interview a few years back he explained, "I don't think the negative propaganda about rap comes from the true black community—it comes from the bourgeois black community, which I hate. Those are the blacks who have an attitude that because I wear a hat and a gold chain, I'm a nigger and they're better than me." Similarly, the former rap group W.C. and the MAAD Circle levelled an even more sustained attack on those they call "bourgeois Negroes." Proclaiming that the Circle's sympathies lie with "poor folks in the slums," lead rapper W.C. derisively wrote off suburban middle-class African Americans as turncoats and cowards.[46]

Even if we are unwilling to call this "class struggle," there is no denying that these young voices are well aware that not all black folks are equally powerless and oppressed. Now that so many urban African Americans are growing up under black mayors and black police officers, they are slowly coming to the conclusion that black politicians and authority figures are as much to blame for the state of the ghetto as their white counterparts. Unlike the "house niggas" of Malcolm's generation, today's black political elite don't need to beg or plead; some of them run the big house. And as long as the status of the "field niggas" remains unchanged, Malcolm's metaphor will continue to articulate the latent class anger that lies muffled beneath a racial blanket.

Notes

4. Bruce Perry, *Malcolm: The Life of a Man Who Changed Black America* (Barrytown, NY: Station Hill Press, 1991), 182.

5. Malcolm X, with Alex Haley, *The Autobiography of Malcolm X* (New York: Grove Press, 1964), 17–42; Perry, *Malcolm*, 40.

10. Malcolm X, *Autobiography*, 43.

11. Malcolm X, *Autobiography*, 59–60. I discuss Malcolm's relationship to the zoot suit culture extensively in "The Riddle of the Zoot: Malcolm Little and Black Cultural Politics During World War II," *Malcolm X: In Our Own Image*, ed. Joe Wood (New York: St. Martin's Press, 1992), 155–67.

16. Malcolm X, *Autobiography*, 40.

17. "Twenty Million Black People . . ." in *Malcolm X: Last Speeches*, 30; Louis Lomax, *When the Word is Given . . . A Report on Elijah Muhammad, Malcolm X, and the Black Muslim World* (Cleveland and New York: The World Publishing Co., 1963), 191.

27. For a brilliant discussion of the importance of self-transformation, see Cornel West, "Malcolm X and Black Rage," *Malcolm X: In Our Own Image*, ed. Joe Wood (New York: St. Martin's Press, 1992), 48–58; and on Cabral, see Amilcar Cabral's *Revolution in Guinea* (New York: Monthly Review Press, 1969), 110, and *National Liberation and Culture*, trans. Maureen Webster (Syracuse: Syracuse University Press, 1970); Jack McCulloch, *In the Twilight of Revolution: The Political Theory of Amilcar Cabral* (London: Zed Books, 1983), 72–74.

28. Malcolm X, *Autobiography*, 36, 38.

29. Karim, *Remembering Malcolm*, 68; Lomax, *When the Word is Given*, 146–47.

30. Lomax, *When the Word is Given*, 155.

34. "America's Gravest Crisis Since the Civil War," *Malcolm X: The Last Speeches*, 64.

35. Perry, *Malcolm*, 221; Lomax, *When the Word is Given*, 79; Karim, *Remembering Malcolm*, 151.

36. Lincoln, *The Black Muslims*, 138–39.

45. One scholar, at least, believes Malcolm was on the verge of seeing the black bourgeoisie's interests as diametrically opposed to that of the black working class. I'm still skeptical, however. See Kevin Ovenden, *Malcolm X: Socialism and Black Nationalism* (London: Bookmarks, 1992), 44.

46. Ice T quoted in Michael Eric Dyson, "The Culture of Hip Hop," *Zeta* (June 1989): 46; Ice T, *The Iceberg/Freedom of Speech . . . Just Watch What You Say* (Sire Records, 1989); see also Ice T, "Radio Suckers," *Power* (Sire Records, 1989) and "This One's For Me," *The Iceberg/Freedom of Speech . . . Just Watch What You Say*; Ice Cube, "Turn off the Radio," *AmeriKKKa's Most Wanted* (Priority Records, 1991); W.C. and the MAAD Circle, *Ain't A Damn Thang Changed* (Priority Records, 1991).

159

Works by Alex Haley and Malcolm X

Alex Haley

The Autobiography of Malcolm X, 1965.

Roots: The Saga of an American Family, 1976.

A Different Kind of Christmas, 1988.

Queen: The Story of an American Family (with David Stevens), 1993.

Mama Flora's Family (with David Stevens), 1998.

Malcolm X

The Autobiography of Malcolm X. With the assistance of Alex Haley, 1965.

Malcolm X Speaks: Selected Speeches and Statements. George Breitman, ed., 1965.

The Speeches of Malcolm X at Harvard. Archie Epps, ed., 1968.

By Any Means Necessary: Speeches, Interviews, and a Letter by Malcolm X. George Breitman, ed., 1970.

The End of White World Supremacy: Four Speeches by Malcolm X. Benjamin Karim, ed., 1971.

The Last Speeches: Malcolm X. Bruce Perry, ed., 1989.

February 1965, The Final Speeches: Malcolm X. Steve Clark, ed., 1992.

Annotated Bibliography

Baldwin, James. *The Fire Next Time*. New York: Dial Press, 1963.

Eloquent essay includes a description of an encounter with Nation of Islam leader Elijah Muhammad. A profound and important literary essay on race in America.

Breitman, George, ed. *Malcolm X Speaks: Selected Speeches and Statements*. New York: Grove Press, 1965.

Collection of Malcolm's speeches made in the last eight tumultuous months of his life after his break with the Black Muslims.

Breitman, George, Herman Porter and Baxter Smith. *The Assassination of Malcolm X*. New York: Pathfinder, 1976.

Firsthand coverage of the Malcolm X assassination trial. Raises questions of a coverup and police involvement.

Gallen, David, ed. *A Malcolm X Reader*. New York: Carroll and Graf, 1994.

A collection of interviews, excerpts from speeches, and reflections on Malcolm X.

———, ed. *Malcolm X: As They Knew Him*. New York: Carroll and Graf, 1992.

Remembrances of Malcolm and explorations of his death and the aftermath, including pieces by Maya Angelou and James Baldwin.

Goldman, Peter. *The Death and Life of Malcolm X*. Urbana: University of Illinois Press, 1979.

Biography by *Newsweek* editor who personally knew Malcolm. Focuses on the last few years of Malcolm's life and describes Malcolm's lasting influence on the black community before and after his death.

hooks, bell. "Malcolm X: The Longed for Feminist Manhood." *Outlaw Culture: Resisting Representations*. New York: Routledge, 1994.

Feminist perspective on the position of black men in society and their attitudes toward black women; this essay addresses Malcolm X's sexism in *The Autobiography*.

Kempton, Daniel. "Writing the Dictionary: The Education of Malcolm X." *The Centennial Review*, vol. 37, no.2 (1992): 253-66.

Kempton analyzes the significance of the role of literacy in Malcolm X's intellectual evolution and political ideologies.

Lincoln, C. Eric. *The Black Muslims in America*. Westport, CT: Greenwood Press, 1973.

Originally published in 1961, this second edition includes updates and a foreword by Gordon W. Allport. An important sociological study of the formation and development of the Black Muslim movement in America.

Ohmann, Carol. "The Autobiography of Malcolm X: The Revolutionary Use of the Franklin Tradition." *American Quarterly*, vol. 22 (1970): 131-49.

An early and important article that compares the autobiographies of Malcolm X and Benjamin Franklin, situating Malcolm's autobiography as a profoundly American autobiography.

Perry, Bruce. *Malcolm: The Life of a Man Who Changed America*. New York: Talman Company, 1991.

Biography that offers a detailed portrait of Malcolm's life. Serves as an interesting text to read alongside the *Autobiography*.

Sales, William. *From Civil Rights to Black Liberation: Malcolm and The Organization of Afro-American Unity*. Boston: South End Press, 1994.

Focuses on Malcolm X's formation of the OAAU and his role as a revolutionary; also examines how the organization grew after his death.

Strickland, William. *Malcolm X: Make it Plain*. New York: Viking, 1994.

Tie-in book to the PBS *American Experience* documentary on Malcolm. Includes photographs, an essay, and snippets by family, close friends, acquaintances, and those that Malcolm X influenced.

Wood, Joe, ed. *Malcolm X: In Our Own Image*. New York: St. Martin's Press, 1992.

A collection of essays by a variety of writers that focus on Malcolm X and his achievements.

X, Malcolm. *By Any Means Necessary (Malcolm X Speeches & Writings)*. 2nd edition. New York: Pathfinder Press, 1992.

Eleven speeches and interviews, in which Malcolm speaks on women's rights, U.S. intervention in the Congo and Vietnam, capitalism and socialism, and American politics.

Contributors

Harold Bloom is Sterling Professor of the Humanities at Yale University. He is the author of 30 books, including *Shelley's Mythmaking*, *The Visionary Company*, *Blake's Apocalypse*, *Yeats*, *A Map of Misreading*, *Kabbalah and Criticism*, *Agon: Toward a Theory of Revisionism*, *The American Religion*, *The Western Canon*, and *Omens of Millennium: The Gnosis of Angels, Dreams, and Resurrection*. *The Anxiety of Influence* sets forth Professor Bloom's provocative theory of the literary relationships between the great writers and their predecessors. His most recent books include *Shakespeare: The Invention of the Human*, a 1998 National Book Award finalist, *How to Read and Why*, *Genius: A Mosaic of One Hundred Exemplary Creative Minds*, *Hamlet: Poem Unlimited*, *Where Shall Wisdom Be Found?*, and *Jesus and Yahweh: The Names Divine*. In 1999, Professor Bloom received the prestigious American Academy of Arts and Letters Gold Medal for Criticism. He has also received the International Prize of Catalonia, the Alfonso Reyes Prize of Mexico, and the Hans Christian Andersen Bicentennial Prize of Denmark.

David P. Demarest, Jr. is a professor of English at Carnegie Mellon University. He is the author of *The River Ran Red*, an anthology commemorating the Homestead Strike of 1892

Paul John Eakin is Ruth N. Halls Professor Emeritus of English at Indiana University. He is the author of *How Our Lives Become Stories: Making Selves* (1999), *Touching the World: Reference in Autobiography* (1992), and *Fictions in Autobiography* (1985).

H. Porter Abbott is emeritus professor of English at the University of California, Santa Barbara. His books include *The Cambridge Introduction to Narrative* and *Diary Fiction: Writing as Action*.

John Edgar Wideman is a professor of English at the University of Massachusetts, Amherst. He has published articles on

Malcolm X, Spike Lee, Denzel Washington, Michael Jordan, and Emmett Till. His many novels and short story collections include *The Lynchers, Hiding Place, Sent for You Yesterday, The Cattle Killing,* and *All Stories Are True.*

Clenora Hudson-Weems is a professor of English at the University of Missouri, Columbia. She is the author of *Africana Womanism: Reclaiming Ourselves* and *Emmett Till: The Sacrificial Lamb of the Civil Rights Movement.*

Carol Tulloch is a research associate at University of the Arts, London, Chelsea.

Celeste Michelle Condit is a professor of speech communications at the University of Georgia. She is coeditor, with John Louis Lucaites and Sally Caudill, of *Contemporary Rhetorical Theory: A Reader* (1999).

John Louis Lucaites is a professor of rhetoric and public culture at Indiana University. His books include *No Caption Needed: Iconic Photographs, Public Culture, and Liberal Democracy* (2007), coauthored with Robert Hariman.

Bashir M. El-Beshti was professor of English at Wake Forest University. He died in 2005.

Maria Josefina Saldaña-Portillo is an associate professor of English at Rutgers University. She is the author of *The Revolutionary Imagination in the Americas and the Age of Development* (2003).

Robin D.G. Kelley is a professor of anthropology at Columbia University. He has published several books, including *Three Strikes: The Fighting Spirit of Labor's Last Century* (coauthored with Howard Zinn and Dana Frank) and *Freedom Dreams: The Black Radical Imagination.*

Acknowledgments

David P. Demarest, Jr., excerpt from *"The Autobiography of Malcolm X*: Beyond Didacticism," from *CLA Journal*, Vol. XVI, no. 2, December 1972: pp. 180–187. Copyright © 1972 by the College Language Association. Used by permission of The College Language Association.

Paul John Eakin, excerpt from "Malcolm X and the Limits of Autobiography." Reprinted from *Criticism*, vol. XVIII, no. 3, Summer (1976), with the permission of Wayne State University Press, Detroit, Michigan 48201-1308. Copyright © 1976.

H. Porter Abbott, excerpt from "Organic Form in the Autobiography of a Convert: The Example of Malcolm X," from *CLA Journal*, vol. XXIII, no. 2, December 1979: pp. 129–137. Copyright © 1980 by the College Language Association. Used by permission of The College Language Association.

John Edgar Wideman, "Malcolm X: The Art of Autobiography," Joe Wood, ed., from *Malcolm X: In Our Own Image*, 1992, New York: St. Martin's Press, reproduced with permission of Palgrave Macmillan.

Clenora Hudson-Weems, excerpt from "From Malcolm Little to El Hajj Malik El Shabazz: Malcolm's Evolving Attitude Toward Africana Women." This article was first published in *The Western Journal of Black Studies*, vol. 17, no. 1, Spring 1993: pp. 27–30. Reprinted with permission.

Carol Tulloch, from" "'My Man, Let Me Pull Your Coat to Something': Malcolm X," from *Fashion Cultures: Theories, Explorations and Analysis*, edited by Stella Bruzzi and Pamela Church Gibson, Copyright © 2000 Stella Bruzzi and Pamela Church Gibson for selection and editorial matter, Individual

Index

conversion to Muslim faith and, 85–87
disintegration of family, 78
father's influence, 78, 81
meetings with Laura and Sophia, 27, 82–83
mother's memory opens door for Haley, 73, 77–81
"pre-Islamic submission," 87–88
teenage dances, 81–82
Organization of Afro-American Unity (OAAU). *See* OAAU
Ostrowski, Mr. (English teacher), 24, 153

P

Pan-Africanism, 137
Perry, Bruce, 99
Pilgrim's Progress evoked by Mecca visit, 59–60
"Pink-poodle" image, 23–24
Pork, prohibition against eating, 79–80, 128
Predictions of own death, 55, 57, 141
Prison, 18, 35–40, 96, 128

R

Race relations in America, 20, 54
Reading, as favorite pastime, 39
Red (pseudonym), 30, 103
Rhetoric, revolutionary, 112–127.
See also Black nationalism; Muslim Mosque, Inc.
  "ballot or the bullet" speech, 113, 123
  constructive rhetoric search, 121–122
  dissenting rhetoric, 116–121
  Harvard Law School speech (1960), 154–155
  limits on, 122–123
  revisionist Black history, 114–116

revival of interest in Malcolm X, 112, 123n1, 157
Roots (Haley), 12, 13
Roseland Ballroom, 104, 151
Rustin, Bayard, 119

S

Saldana-Portillo, Maria Josefiña, 138–149
Sammy the Pimp, 17, 30–31, 32, 42
Separatism of blacks espoused by Malcolm, 46
Seventh-Day Adventists, 22, 23, 79
Shabazz, Betty (wife). *See* Sister Betty (wife)
Shawarbi, Mahmoud Youssef, 51
Shorty, 16, 25–26, 34–35, 103
Sister Betty (wife)
  character overview, 15
  on Malcolm's apparent change after Mecca, 132
  on Malcolm's philosophy on women, 101
  marriage to Malcolm, 43–44
Sophia (white girlfriend)
  character overview, 16
  first meeting with, 82–83
  loyalty to Malcolm, 33–34
  as Malcolm's partner in crime, 34–35
  marriage of, 31, 33–34
  as status symbol, 27, 29, 95
Speeches, revolutionary. *See* Rhetoric, revolutionary
Structure of *Autobiography*, 18–19, 59, 66–67
Summary and analysis. *See* Analysis and summary
Sunni Islam, 7
Swerlin family, 23

T

Tanzania African National Union (TANU), 99